Published in February 2022

ISBN: 978-1-910505-75-5

Translated by Michael Janiec
Edited by Mark Hughes
Designed by Richard Parsons

Printed and bound in Bosnia and Herzegovina by GPS

Published by Evro Publishing
Westrow House, Holwell, Sherborne, Dorset DT9 5LF, UK

www.evropublishing.com

Front cover Max during 2021, the year that brought 10 Grand Prix victories and the World Championship crown. **Back cover** Max wins his home race, the Dutch Grand Prix, in the Red Bull RB16B. **Frontispiece** Last-gasp victory in Abu Dhabi made him 2021 World Champion.

MAX

THE DUTCH MASTER

THE UNAUTHORISED BIOGRAPHY OF MAX VERSTAPPEN

PUBLISHING

ANDRÉ HOOGEBOOM

CONTENTS

PROLOGUE
A WINNER
ABOVE ALL

Like a true Dutch Master, Max Verstappen has revitalised Formula 1, rewritten the rules, made the sport more exciting — and put the Netherlands on the motorsport map. The extent of his influence cannot be underestimated. Formula 1 is an international sport, appealing to young and old, modern in nature, dynamic, ruthlessly competitive — and a political snake pit as well. Even so, arriving in 2015 as a 17-year-old, he seemed to feel at home immediately, quickly producing impressive performances, tentative at first, later with conviction. By 2021, such a momentous season, he really was stringing together the pole positions and victories, culminating in him becoming World Champion after that dramatic last lap at that dramatic last race.

His face is recognised across the globe. He's close to reaching the status of a Messiah in his home country, where his prominence as a sports superstar now matches that of another JC, the footballer Johan Cruyff. In 2021, indeed, he surpassed the great Cruyff's achievements when he won the Formula 1 World Championship, a pinnacle that even the Dutch footballing hero didn't quite manage to emulate in 1974 when the World Cup Final was lost to West Germany.

From the moment when Max's father, Jos Verstappen, first entered him in professional karting competition, winning the World Championship was always his ambition. Whereas Cruyff saw playing the finest football as his objective, the Verstappens, father and son, only aspired to the ultimate accolade of the Formula 1 crown. Just winning races was never enough. All that counts at the end of a long season is the world title. And one title also isn't enough. The hunger for success will only truly be satiated when multiple World Championships have been won.

Max has brought the Netherlands into unprecedented prominence in international motorsport. Until his first win in Barcelona in 2016, Dutch racing drivers had played merely supporting roles in their sport. Memorable successes had only really been achieved at Le Mans, with Gijs van Lennep and Jan Lammers, who had both won the prestigious 24-hour race. In Formula 1 the Dutch were known only for crashing and circulating as backmarkers.

Max's influence has been so huge that the Netherlands actually got its Grand Prix back. Menno de Jong, co-owner of the Zandvoort circuit, which returned to the Formula 1 calendar in 2021 after a 36-year absence, is honest about this: 'Without Max there wouldn't be a Dutch Grand Prix and without him it wouldn't make sense to host one.'

Above all, Max Verstappen is here to stay as a 24-year-old World Champion, with perhaps more than a decade still left at the top. He has said he would be satisfied with three world titles, which would place him with some of the very best in the sport's history: Jack Brabham, Jackie Stewart, Nelson Piquet and Ayrton Senna each won three, while Alain Prost and Sebastian Vettel — strangely, you could almost forget him — both have four. Conceivably, he could finish with seven or more, enabling him to follow in the footsteps of two of the greatest racers ever — Michael Schumacher and Lewis Hamilton. But many variables and unpredictable factors lie ahead: regulation changes, technical difficulties, bad luck...

In the Netherlands, Max's small entourage was soon convinced of his qualities. Elsewhere, David Coulthard quickly became a big fan. Journalists Peter Windsor and Will Buxton were also in no doubt, especially the latter, who saw young Max excel at the age of 16 in an American racing category. Sir Jackie Stewart knows how to handle the pressure of performing at the very highest level: 'Mind management is the most important thing in this sport. He does that well, although he was a bit wild in his first years.'

Verstappen has become one of the greats, whether or not he goes on to win more world titles. But Sir Jackie's adage is set in stone, as he knows better than anyone: 'To finish first, you first have to finish.' In other words, you don't become World Champion in the first corner.

In some ways Verstappen has liberated the sport from a rather dull predictability, only to exchange it for — oh, the irony — a new predictability. This is because, despite all of the young Dutchman's memorable races and passing manoeuvres, he prefers to confine his overtaking to backmarkers and, as in Austria and Mexico during his 2021 campaign, rush to victory unchallenged. As an old associate confirms in this book: 'Give Max a good car and he will drive away from the whole field after the start. They won't see him again until after the race'. Max confirms this: 'That's how I like to see it.'

Bernie Ecclestone, Formula 1's long-time tsar, noted with pleasure in mid-2021 that Lewis Hamilton's time was up. Ecclestone remembered that Michael Schumacher's dominance did Formula 1 more harm than good. Sport thrives on the rapid succession of heroes. While statistical accumulation looks pleasing, this adulation of superheroes shouldn't last too long, or it will end up becoming a dictatorship. A hero who falls off his pedestal has much more publicity value and therefore financial value. Bernie has always had money in mind. That's how he became one of Britain's richest men.

Verstappen's progress since entering Formula 1 with Toro Rosso as a youth has been phenomenal. In 2015, his first year, he finished 12th in the World Championship standings. He followed that with fifth in 2016 (mainly with Red Bull), sixth in 2017 (a year that brought seven retirements), fourth in 2018, and third in 2019 and 2020 (using the highly reliable new Honda engine that didn't break down once). His rise was brutally interrupted in 2020 by the pandemic, which put the whole world on hold, before resuming in 2021. By the end of 2021 he had won a total of 20 Formula 1 Grands Prix, 10 of them during his World Championship-winning season.

Formula 1 loves records and lists. There is a record for every facet of the sport. Verstappen has already collected a staggering number:

- Youngest driver to start a Grand Prix: Australia 2015, 17 years 166 days
- Youngest driver to score points in a Grand Prix: Malaysia 2015, 17 years 180 days
- Youngest driver to lead a Grand Prix: Spain 2016, 18 years 228 days
- Youngest driver on a Grand Prix podium: Spain 2016, 18 years 228 days
- Youngest Grand Prix winner: Spain 2016, 18 years 228 days
- Youngest driver to set fastest lap in a Grand Prix: Brazil 2016, 19 years 44 days
- Youngest grand slam winner (pole position, fastest lap, victory and leading all race laps): Austria 2021, 23 years 277 days

A taste of what lies ahead: 12-year-old Max visits the
2009 German Grand Prix with father Jos.

Few observers and fans of the sport were convinced of his talent as early as 2015, when he débuted at the age of 17. They thought back smugly to father Jos, who was also fast, but rather impetuous. Here was a kid, the son of a driver who had spent 10 years stubbornly grinding his teeth against the reality of Formula 1 with only occasional success. Seventeen years old? Come on!

But they hadn't seen how, in relative anonymity, Verstappen Junior and Senior had forged an enormously strong bond. The father soon knew the quality of the son's pedigree and — perhaps just as importantly — knew from experience exactly how things had to be done on the path to Formula 1.

In his younger days, Max was an uncut diamond, but Verstappen Senior and his immediate circle soon saw the potential. Paul Lemmens, owner of the famous karting track in Genk, watched young Max grow up at his facility, and saw how father and son — he had also known Jos as a boy — conducted themselves. He recognised champion material. As a seven-year-old, Max drove his first kart race and immediately became champion in the 'minis'. Lemmens noticed, too, how well father and son got on with each other. Max was never pushed. In fact, he was often the one who didn't know when to stop. He would shout to Jos: 'Come on Dad, another lap.' He was patiently tutored by a professional coaching team that included Huub Rothengatter, Jos's former manager. He was meticulously prepared for the big time.

Early in 2014, Max went to the United States to drive in the Florida Winter Series, a relatively obscure competition. It was Team Verstappen's idea. This was still a tight-knit circle that comprised just Jos Verstappen, Huub Rothengatter and Raymond Vermeulen — and Max. With precious little media attention, the four of them attended this four-round race series in the warmth of Florida in February, a month in which European circuit racing is at a standstill. Jos, ambitious as he had been as a racing driver, had himself abandoned European winters for New Zealand summers, an exercise that cost a lot and yielded little more than experience.

In Florida there was a moment when Max wasn't paying attention and drove into a stationary car in the pitlane. That was a financial headache for Team Verstappen, which was far from flush. Who was going to pay for the considerable damage? The father had spent years training his son and no longer had any income from racing. The piggy bank suddenly looked rather empty.

Jos had earned plenty of money in Formula 1. He had driven for good teams and had had an effective manager who knew how to find the best way through the financial maze of motorsport. But in nurturing his son's career,

Verstappen Senior had been burning through his reserves. Max's karting career had cost a fortune and Dad had paid for it all. There had been little revenue and plenty of expenditure. Jos did everything himself: driving to the circuits, paying for the petrol, tuning the kart, making it competitive — a craft in which he excelled, by the way, and that could easily have been a livelihood for him. But in choosing to invest in Max, there was always the possibility that the money would run out. And climbing the motor racing ladder costs a lot of money — potentially millions. Ayrton Senna, for example, came from a truly wealthy Brazilian family and was able to travel to Europe and make his name at his father's expense.

In the Netherlands there was no crock of gold available to take a promising young driver towards the big time. In addition, a disadvantage of working quietly, in relative anonymity, had been an absence of publicity to help bring in money. So when Max drove into the back of that car in Florida, because he was checking data on his steering wheel, the damage amounted to many thousands of dollars. There was some cursing in private but Max wasn't criticised for it. Verstappen Senior later said in a documentary: 'Max shouldn't hold back because he might cause damage; if you do that, you can't race.'

The adventure in America brought masses of experience, including the political side. Jos knew about the political element in Formula 1, where the 'Piranha Club' — the most powerful and influential figures in the paddock — call the shots. When at Benetton, Verstappen Senior had had to deal with Flavio Briatore, The Godfather of Formula 1. 'It is no secret,' remembers journalist David Tremayne, 'that at Benetton they drove two different cars. One for Jos and the faster one for Michael [Schumacher].'

Before the Florida trip, Max had already had an impressive test session in a Formula Renault car. Also carried out in deep secrecy, this opportunity was provided by one of the family's racing connections, Sander Dorsman, owner of the MP Motorsport team. The test took place in Britain, at the Pembrey circuit in South Wales. Pembrey is a somewhat primitive place, where the tarmac is imbued with the smell of fuel, and the pits garages often contain the oil-soaked rags of previous occupants. It could be a track from a bygone era, romantic in a way, a haven for nostalgic souls. Here young Max drove his first laps in a single-seater racing car. He performed so well that engineer Tony Shaw sometimes still wakes up in the middle of the night, recalling it vividly. He told Dorsman that he had never seen such talent.

It went unnoticed elsewhere. Only the insiders registered the significance.

No one in the Netherlands had any idea. How could they? Since the loss of Zandvoort from the Formula 1 calendar after the 1985 Dutch Grand Prix, and Jos's departure from Formula 1 at the end of 2003, motor racing had been almost entirely overlooked by the Dutch media. The advantage of this for Max was absence of hype. While various young footballers with an ounce of talent were labelled as the 'next Johan Cruyff', nobody noticed this nurturing of a motorsport genius.

The next step in Max's career would be a very important one — but what should it be? Here was a karting world champion with Formula 1 potential and yet he was still very young. Managers and clubs queue up for talented young footballers and their agents promise riches. Of course, young Max's future looked similarly bright, but instead of making money for Team Verstappen, so far he had only cost them.

Max had to make a move that would lead quickly to success, otherwise everything achieved so far would have been in vain. Team Verstappen had the advantage of a strong network. Everyone knew Jos — and Jos knew everyone. In Formula 1 it's often more about who you know than who you are.

Stepping into Formula Renault, the most logical next step on the ladder, wasn't good enough for Max's entourage. Formula 3 looked a much better option but cost a lot of money. A ride with the renowned racing stable of Frits van Amersfoort, where big names like Charles Leclerc and Mick Schumacher, as well as numerous promising Dutch drivers and indeed father Jos, had enjoyed their apprenticeships, was extremely expensive. For a while, the teenager's future hung by a thread. Until Huub Rothengatter personally pulled out his wallet and paid the bill.

People in the Netherlands were still oblivious. The phenomenon of Max Verstappen, who just a few years later would set the entire country on fire, drove impressive races in an invisible class, in a championship he didn't even win. Only local newspapers — those in his home province of Limburg that had been following him since he was a little boy — noticed that something special was going on.

But then again, how many talented kart drivers in Formula Renault and Formula 3 ever manage to get within sight of the harbour before they sink?

The sources I have quoted in this book, experts and specialists, came up with so many decisive arguments about Max Verstappen's talent that my own professional scepticism as a journalist — see first, then believe

Max receives an orange ovation as he wins the 2021 Dutch Grand Prix.

— soon evaporated. Yes, Max was a special boy. In all classes on his way to Formula 1, he was effectively invincible.

From the countless experts I have spoken to when writing about Formula 1 in general, and Max Verstappen in particular, I have heard nothing but words of admiration and respect. And that goes for the persevering father as well as his supremely talented son — but of course the evidence is irrefutable.

Max was always truly committed, a boy whose outlook wasn't clouded by any of the other temptations in modern life. When he stepped into a go-kart at the age of four, there was only one direction to go: straight ahead, with no side turnings. He lived a monomaniacal life of racing and travelling — and he wanted nothing else.

Jos repeatedly said that he would have liked his son to play football but Max chose karting. As long as he did it with heart and soul, that was the father's only rule. An unnecessary rule, as it turned out. Young Max didn't even want to play football, because he couldn't win. And winning was and remains his focus. Verstappens don't like to lose.

Max was guided by an experienced father who didn't need to convince him. Unlike fellow countryman and Wimbledon winner Richard Krajicek, who spoke out after his active career about his father Petr's overbearing control, almost a reign of terror, Verstappen Junior never arrived late for 'work'.

Perhaps this makes it seem as if it all came naturally, but this isn't entirely true. This only applied to the things within their control — the driving, the car set-up, the race strategy. The financial aspect was a different matter.

Jos Verstappen not only had a good understanding of Formula 1 and its financial side but had also been advised by racing entrepreneur Huub Rothengatter. Jos's own path through Formula 1 had been marked by pitfalls, because it was always more about money than anything else, such as how fast he was — or could have been with the right equipment.

In Max's climb up the ladder, financial independence was a vital factor for success. Not only did Senior pave the way for Junior's career, but he tied his own material future to it. However, the risk Jos took in doing so wasn't excessive because he had no doubt about Max's glittering potential. In contrast, many father/son racing relationships involve a blind spot.

Frits van Amersfoort knows all about this. He has encountered many fathers who have been willing to go into deep debt to help their offspring start careers in racing only to find that the talent wasn't there in sufficient abundance.

It was in Max's case.

Every insider who saw young Max at work was captivated by his wondrous ability. But talent alone doesn't pay the bills. So Verstappen Junior, in effect, had to pull out his own credit card to pay for his seat in van Amersfoort's racing team. With a little help, the balance was just enough to get him started in Formula 3. This was a big, decisive step that would have been too much of a stretch for drivers with less ability. Promising young drivers usually start in a lesser category such as Formula Ford or Formula Renault. Ayrton Senna, for example, started in Formula Ford.

In 2015 Max proved what he was capable of. The Formula 3 race for Van Amersfoort Racing at the Norisring put him on the radar of Helmut Marko, senior executive at Red Bull, former racing driver and noted talent scout. This sealed his future. Marko observed a 16-year-old whom he felt sure could handle a Formula 1 car. The young Verstappen was still somewhat lanky and boyish, his shoulders seemingly not yet broad enough to control 700 horsepower. His lean face was pimply and he didn't yet need to shave.

And yet, within five years, this young adolescent matured into a world star with mastery over all aspects of celebrity life.

He hasn't been blinded by the hype that has surrounded him. Max has remained an authentic individual, a Verstappen. He has grown up politically, picks his moments behind the microphone, and knows the effect of words. Sometimes a hint of Jos shines through in occasional sporting frustration. Max's media appearances are a mirror of his soul.

That has gone wrong on occasions, as at the United States Grand Prix in 2017, when he called a steward a 'retard' for losing a podium place. He even did 'community service' — assisting at a Formula E race in Marrakesh in Morocco — after shoving long-time rival Esteban Ocon in front of the cameras in *parc fermé* at the Brazilian Grand Prix of 2018. Incidents like this haven't been repeated because he has become older, smarter and — yes — more political too. The diamond is almost ready, cut and of high carat.

The dot on the horizon — his ultimate goal of Formula 1 — gradually became an exclamation mark, within grasp at last. The first experts who had seen him up close were quickly convinced that Max Verstappen was a special kid. The general public followed after the historic victory on 15th May 2016 in Barcelona.

Since then, Max Verstappen has been ever-present in his home country's media as well as ever-more-prominent around the globe. In the Netherlands, no-one else gets more coverage in newspapers and magazines, and on television, social media and countless websites.

His fan base has grown enormously. His supporters — 'the orange army' of his Limburg homeland — show up all over the world. They have witnessed victories in Austria, where the Red Bull Ring turns orange every year, and made trips to the desert venues in the Middle East. Orange has surpassed Ferrari red as the dominant colour in many grandstands.

'That passion of the Dutch is fantastic,' Sir Jackie Stewart observed. 'It has given colour back to Formula 1.' The Dutch fans outnumber the followers of other Formula 1 drivers. The fact that Max Verstappen regularly becomes 'Driver of the Day' is due not only to his performances on the track but also his enormous popularity among the Dutch spectators who vote for him *en masse*.

Holland loves Verstappen as it once loved Johan Cruyff. The heyday of Dutch football, with Cruyff as its icon, was more or less taken for granted in the 1970s, when Dutch teams reached new and subsequently unmatched heights with four consecutive European Cup victories (one for Feyenoord of Rotterdam in 1970, then three for Ajax of Amsterdam) and two consecutive World Cup Finals (in 1974 and 1978).

The same couldn't be said about Dutch motorsport, which had never had any sort of heyday. In 2015, when Max made his Formula 1 début, motor racing was rather an afterthought in the minds of Dutch sports fans. The national circuit, Zandvoort, looked somewhat faded amidst the dunes of its seaside location. Motorsport in the Netherlands was just a footnote in the big world of Formula 1, a sub-culture for a handful of petrolheads and diehards, the fanatics who still watched the races on television even during the dullest periods of Michael Schumacher's domination. After all, what was the point of following Formula 1 without a national favourite? For the best part of 20 years sports purists judged the races boring parades, usually involving a German winner (Schumacher, Vettel, Mercedes).

With Max Verstappen, everything changed. He signed up for a 'Year Zero' of Dutch motorsport. Not only because he was so talented, and managed to win in the unknown territory of an unloved sport, and shook up the established order, but also because he's cut from cloth that appeals to his countrymen. He's an uncompromising attacker. The Netherlands loves that. A small country punching above its weight. The underdog with its chest out.

Verstappen is all that in one. He's the personification of the Dutch spirit: assertive, aggressive, enterprising, ambitious and — above all — a winner.

Lewis Hamilton congratulates Max after losing out to him
in the 2021 Abu Dhabi Grand Prix.

PART 1
CLIMBING THE LADDER

CHAPTER 1
FIRST STEPS IN FORMULA 1

I t's 3rd October 2014. A self-conscious young man walks through the paddock at the Suzuka circuit in Japan. He's carrying an enormous helmet, like a knight on his way to a tournament. He's wearing a thin, dark grey hoodie bearing the emblem of Toro Rosso/Red Bull, with a white T-shirt underneath. On his head is a regular Red Bull cap, of the type that can be bought at numerous merchandise stores. He would blend in on the streets of any European town.

He's 17, still with some acne. He has no sign of facial hair but carries himself like a grown man. Maybe he could pass for 19 — but no older.

At cold, dank Suzuka, a difficult and historic track, he walks past the still-closed garages and pits. His gaze is focused at a target on the horizon — a target he identified silently, with his father, years earlier.

As he lowers himself into the Toro Rosso's cockpit, he allows himself a smile — albeit a slightly wry one. Right now, he's doing something millions of 17-year-olds around the world dream of: he's getting into a real Formula 1 car. The smile conceals his inner exuberance. The dream has become reality.

Slowly, he drops into the custom-fitted seat and stretches his legs into the cramped compartment ahead. This is where the pedals are — where the power resides. A gentle push on the accelerator pedal conjures approximately 700 horsepower in a car weighing about 700 kilograms. A power-to-weight ratio of one-to-one. He's aware of what can happen once this amount of power is unleashed onto the tarmac. It's a force that requires the greatest respect.

You have to be a man to tame and wield this power correctly. A toreador. But this driver isn't a man yet. He's still an adolescent. He's Max Verstappen.

Media people surround him after his first experience of those 700 horses. You could almost feel sorry for him, so young and inexperienced in this situation, accosted by a crowd of journalists with cameras, recorders and notebooks. His father educated him in all sorts of different subjects, but media training was hardly on the agenda. How can you arm yourself against such superior numbers? He should still be at school, listening to his teachers, working towards those exams that will help him get on in life.

Now, here in Japan with Suzuka's characteristic Ferris wheel in the background, he's speaking to dozens of journalists who eagerly absorb every syllable. In his home country, this historic moment passes largely unnoticed because the mainstream media barely covers it. The last Dutch driver of any note in Formula 1 was his father, a man with 107 Grand Prix starts to his name. After Jos Verstappen, Formula 1 in the Netherlands went on the back burner.

Internationally, this teenager is a curiosity. Nobody knows quite how to interpret this. What is a boy like this doing here? What can a boy like this do? Yes, he's Jos's son, and that means something. Journalists who have done their homework know where he comes from. They know he was a superb kart racer who dominated every race he entered. They know Jos was rather a sensation, an attacker, a somewhat wild driver. Those with any sense of history know about the big crash with Eddie Irvine that ended Jos's first Formula 1 race, driving for Benetton alongside Michael Schumacher in Brazil in 1994, available on YouTube for all to see — and to realise that it wasn't Jos's fault. To sum up, they know that this Max comes from a good home.

Other sons have followed their fathers into Formula 1, from Jacques Villeneuve to Nico Rosberg, from Damon Hill to Nelson Piquet Jr. Kevin Magnussen, too, and Carlos Sainz Jr. In fact there have been 14 such sons. But none was as young as Jos Verstappen's son.

Max's freshness charms the crowd. It's striking: he doesn't seem to care. He performs on this stage, one that's normally far too big for a 17-year-old, as if it's the most natural thing in the world. He was born for the racetrack, just as Johan Cruyff was born for the football pitch.

He gives spontaneous answers to probing questions from the international journalists. He was four years old when he insisted his father buy a real

His first appearance in a Formula 1 car — Toro Rosso, Suzuka, Japan, 2014.

The assured 16-year-old settles into the cockpit
of a Formula 1 car for the first time.

go-kart. He already wanted to race but wasn't allowed to because he was too young. Six years old was early enough, judged his father. But even a young Verstappen doesn't like to be told what to do. He kept insisting. Six months later he was allowed to have a go-kart. His father must have been secretly proud. Such a small boy, already so eager. Was there already a dot on the horizon? Or was it still a father/son thing?

In this book several interviewees say that there were talks about the 'Verstappen Project' from day one. That father, when Max was in the cradle, already saw him in a Formula 1 car. Some sceptics say Max had to fulfil the ambition that his father never achieved, although there's no evidence for this. According to those who know the relationship, no compulsion was involved. Max's motorsport education was hard but fair. It was all he wanted to do. There was no need for any coercion.

As a baby, Finnish footballer Jari Litmanen slept with a football in his cradle. That would have been difficult with a go-kart, but maybe for Max his cradle actually was a go-kart, with a teething ring for a steering wheel. It just might have been.

On the professional karting scene there's a sub-culture of hundreds of keen fathers. They all dream of Formula 1 careers for their sons. But they aren't called Verstappen. They don't have the same racing genes. That very special DNA simply isn't present.

In the upcoming chapters we retrace Max Verstappen's roots in the Netherlands and in Belgium. We get to know Paul Lemmens, the owner of the karting track in Genk who saw not only Max (and his father) emerge, but also three past World Champions — Michael Schumacher of Germany, Kimi Räikkönen of Finland and Jenson Button of Britain. Lemmens raised karting to a higher level in the Benelux countries by managing a track that meets international standards. Genk is the birthplace of champions and Paul Lemmens is their patriarch.

Then we'll continue with Kees van de Grint, a good friend of Jos. He was the confidant and friend of seven-times World Champion Michael Schumacher and also played a modest role at the start of Jos's career. When he was working for Schumacher at Ferrari, he gave clandestine advice to Jos in the paddock.

Sander Dorsman, team manager at MP Motorsport, was instrumental in Max's ascent to Formula 1. Just like Frits van Amersfoort of VAR (Van Amersfoort Racing), Dorsman's team is a springboard for young talent aiming for Formula 1. When Max drove his first single-seater at Pembrey in Wales, in pouring rain and in secret, it was in a car run by MP Motorsport.

Dennis van de Laar drove with Max in the Ferrari Driver Academy Florida Winter Series at the beginning of 2014. Van de Laar is quite unusual in that karting played no part in his racing ambitions. Another unusual thing about him is that he beat Max in his first single-seater race against him — but never again. Van de Laar invested a lot in motorsport and believed for a long time that Formula 1 was achievable but racing against Max — and some other top talents — was such a sobering experience that he gave up and instead followed in his father's footsteps, becoming a successful entrepreneur.

British Formula 1 journalist Will Buxton also got to drive against Max and became one of the first people in the mainstream media to introduce him to a wider audience. This adventure in the 'Sunshine State' was not only instructive but also entertaining.

Then Frits van Amersfoort reflects for us on young Max. A long-time Formula 3 entrant, he not only gave the youngster his first season of single-seater racing, in the 2014 FIA European Formula 3 Championship, but also experienced success with Jos. If you have raced for van Amersfoort's team, the prospect of a glorious career in motor racing becomes a lot brighter.

The Netherlands was soon in the grip of Max Mania after he got into Formula 1, and especially after his first Grand Prix victory, in Spain in May 2016. A couple of weeks later, the 18-year-old's demonstration run with his Red Bull RB12 at Zandvoort was attended by 100,000 fans. The roads to and from the seaside resort were blocked for hours, with more visitors than had ever turned out for the heyday of the Dutch Grand Prix between the 1950s and the 1980s. Only one previous sporting celebration on Dutch soil had attracted more people: that was in 1988 when the national football team was welcomed home after winning the European Championship.

Max Verstappen has been everywhere in Holland ever since, for example as the poster boy for supermarket chain Jumbo or through extensive television coverage from major cable network Ziggo. This, among other things, shows how popular the sport of speed has become in his home country. Although there may be plenty of truth in the perception that Formula 1 is a money-grubbing hobby for the super-rich, a procession of millionaires sponsored by billionaires, it's remarkable that some of the main protagonists have emerged from simple backgrounds.

Youngsters in karting, the best of whom become the stars of Formula 1, come from all social classes, as Paul Lemmens can testify. He took care of Jenson Button for a while and was amazed by his work ethic: 'He was even willing to skip his favourite dessert.' Motorsport also requires drivers to be athletes and no-one, no matter how rich, can spring any surprises without being strong and super-fit. Dennis van de Laar confesses: 'At one point my neck muscles were so strained that I couldn't move my head anymore — I could only lean against the edge of the cockpit.'

That, too, is an element in this Verstappen saga: his athleticism, even when just 17 years old, before he had fully matured physically, has always been at the necessary level.

To illustrate what a Formula 1 driver's body is exposed to, the Singapore street circuit is a good yardstick. Max's big rival, Lewis Hamilton, described it like this: 'Imagine being in a sauna, wearing fireproof overalls and a helmet, and then walking around and doing push-ups.' Max's former Red Bull team-mate, Daniel Ricciardo, also has Singapore observations: 'It's so hot in the car that your sports drink is already as hot as tea at the start. In the cockpit the temperature is around 60 degrees Celsius.'

The number of bends at the Singapore track, 23, is more than at any other current Formula 1 circuit. The drivers are severely tested because there isn't a moment's rest. Braking, accelerating, braking, accelerating… all while being shaken as if in a washing machine because the track is very bumpy. The noise reflected from the walls, fences and buildings is deafening and exhausting. A driver sweats many litres and cannot take in liquid fast enough to mitigate this. According to brake manufacturer Brembo, the force required on the brake pedal at the Singapore Grand Prix is 81.435 kilograms, whereas the figure for the Chinese Grand Prix at Shanghai, which is known as a 'light' circuit in terms of braking, is 'only' 51.353 kilograms. Singapore is a hell for Formula 1 drivers.

Could a 17-year-old handle that? This was a legitimate question from the critics in 2015. That year's Singapore Grand Prix marked Max's coming of age. It was the race of his much-talked-about 'No'. The race in which he adamantly refused to obey Toro Rosso's order to make way for team-mate Carlos Sainz Jr and was praised for it afterwards. His father glowed with pride. This was the moment his son proved that all the teaching hadn't been in vain: 'If he had done it, he would have had a problem with me.'

That doesn't alter the fact that a 17-year-old is still developing. Even Max

Verstappen didn't escape these laws of nature. He was just a boy, with some physical limitations. His muscles weren't fully developed. His brain wasn't yet at its peak. It was widely thought by the establishment that the Max of 2015 wasn't actually ready physically for the big time. But there was one big difference when comparing him with his adolescent peers. A difference that a few factored into their early judgements.

He is a Verstappen.

CHAPTER 2
REIGNING IN SPAIN

O n 15th May 2016, a Dutch teenager rewrote motorsport history. At the Circuit de Catalunya, near Barcelona, he became not only the youngest driver ever to win a Formula 1 Grand Prix but also the only 18-year-old to do so.

This amazing landmark marked the end of one journey and the beginning of another.

His education, undertaken for so long by father Jos with commitment and love, was finally completed in Barcelona — and achieved with a diploma, a trophy and an official presentation. A few days prior to this race Jos had announced that he would retire as a full-time tutor: Max was where he needed to be and henceforth he would manage on his own. Junior proved Senior right. In a race that brought people in the Netherlands and fans around the world to the edge of their seats, he toppled Formula 1's established order in a car he 'still had to get used to'.

Seasoned observers struggled for the right words to describe Max's heroic victory. Former driver and TV commentator David Coulthard, a true Verstappen fan, shouted on British television: 'Forget Leicester City's championship in the Premier League. As far as I am concerned, the victory of 18-year-old Max Verstappen is the story of the year.'

Peter Windsor, long-time journalist and former manager of Nigel Mansell, was stunned by what he saw, covering it extensively on his YouTube channel and speaking of 'the birth of a new star'. It became one of that year's most

The Russian Grand Prix of 2016 was Max's last race in a Toro Rosso.
After that came elevation to the 'senior' team — Red Bull.

watched Formula 1 videos. 'A lot of people thought I had gone over the top,' Windsor told me. 'I didn't think so then and I still don't. Reality today has proved me right. I thought — and still do — that a new era had begun with that victory. The era of Max.'

Will Buxton, Formula 1 media personality and one of the first journalists to see Max in action as a single-seater racer in Florida, has never forgotten that beautiful sunny day in Barcelona: 'Stunning, magical, sensational. Even if those Mercedes cars hadn't run each other off the track, it would have been a wonderful story, because he would have ended up on the podium anyway. But now it became a fairytale.'

Max Verstappen was suddenly a world star, propelled onwards by the Red Bull RB12, a car that he had driven for only a few hours.

For several years, Max judged the 2016 Spanish Grand Prix as his finest victory. On that spring day, he stepped out of anonymity forever and was hailed as the successor to the greats of the sport. The new Ayrton Senna, Michael Schumacher, Lewis Hamilton. A racing phenomenon.

The seed for this flowering had been planted earlier. It went back to the Russian Grand Prix, where Daniil Kvyat disgraced himself at the start of the race by driving his Red Bull into the back of Sebastian Vettel's Ferrari. It marked the end of Kvyat's career as a Red Bull driver: whether the incident at his home race was the straw that broke the camel's back, or just a convenient opportunity to swap him for Verstappen, depends on who you listen to.

Whatever, Team Verstappen, in which father Jos played such an important role, had become impatient. Max had been driving for Toro Rosso for just over a year, having completed a full 2015 season with the team and a handful of early races in 2016. Toro Rosso was uncompetitive and good results were scarce. The Verstappens weren't used to that. Max had always won everywhere, or at least battled for victory. With a Toro Rosso, this was impossible. Without some change, there seemed to be a risk that he could get stuck in mid-pack.

May 2016 became a crazy month for Max Verstappen, starting in Sochi. The Russian Grand Prix on 1st May was a regular race, to the extent that a certain predictable routine was starting to creep in. Verstappen made it through the final qualifying knock-out and placed the Toro Rosso ninth on the grid.

The Toro Rosso, powered by a 2015 Ferrari engine, was nearing its limit. The 2016 season's first three races had brought very little reward. Max qualified for them somewhere in the top ten, then drove around behind the front-runners, occasionally picking up places when others dropped out. The results in these first three races went like this: Australia, qualified fifth, finished tenth; Bahrain, qualified tenth, finished sixth; China, qualified ninth, finished eighth. All rather mediocre, with no improvement.

In Russia it was much the same. He qualified ninth and retired from the race with engine trouble while running sixth.

Kvyat, meanwhile, had made it onto the podium in China with a fine third place. He outplayed Ferrari driver Sebastian Vettel in that race and was praised for a cheeky passing manoeuvre. Fourteen days later, however, the Russian had a nightmarish race in his homeland. Driving like a novice, he tapped Vettel's Ferrari twice on its rear wing at consecutive corners on the first lap. The second instance was worse, for Kvyat's error sent Vettel spinning off into the barrier and resulted in damage to several other cars, including Daniel Ricciardo's sister Red Bull. The mayhem required the race to be stopped. As a consequence, the Red Bull team performed badly after the restart, its two RB12s finishing just 11th (Ricciardo) and 15th (Kvyat).

Red Bull's Helmut Marko had seen enough. Kvyat had been under fire for some time because of disappointing performances and lack of progress. Now Marko intervened decisively. He demoted Kvyat to the 'junior' team, Toro Rosso, and elevated Verstappen to the 'senior' team, Red Bull. With TAG-Heuer (Renault) power, the RB12 was a faster car, with a better chassis.

Suddenly, the cards were reshuffled. Again, discussion arose about whether Max's promotion was premature, and indeed whether his presence in Formula 1 had also come too soon. In addition, could he handle the pressure? Failure, as Marko had already made clear in the media, would result in being shown the door. Kvyat had experienced this but was lucky to be able at least to remain in Formula 1 with a seat at Toro Rosso.

Three years earlier, Max Verstappen had still been driving around in a kart. Now he had one of the fastest cars in the world at his fingertips. His tender age was no longer an excuse. He had really grown up.

A bizarre period followed in which the teenager was completely absorbed in the transition to the top team. He tempered his overly excited responses with a maturity that suited his new status. It was, he said, a totally different car. He had to get used to it. Many procedures were different, the steering

History in the making: Max during the 2016 Spanish Grand Prix at Catalunya.

First to greet victorious Max as he climbed from the
cockpit in Spain was Helmut Marko.

wheel — with all those buttons — seemed a bit more complicated. A podium? Perhaps. Let's see how it goes.

Was he sandbagging to the media, holding his cards close to his chest? Was he downplaying it? Did he know in his heart that it would be all right? That he would get into a new car, get used to the procedures and the steering wheel on Friday and Saturday, then drive the race as he had always done, only now with a faster and better car?

Perhaps. Maybe he was much more confident than he wanted the outside world to believe. It sounds ridiculous, but it doesn't seem to matter to Max Verstappen whether he's driving a complicated state-of-the-art racing machine crammed with sophisticated electronics, or a basic go-kart.

Once again, the 18-year-old's calm approach to the new adventure was striking. In the 2020 documentary film *Whatever It Takes*, which was produced by Team Verstappen, he provides glimpses into his soul. He even allows some human weakness to show, perhaps most notably in a scene in which he comes home rather drunk after a party.

The biggest message in *Whatever It Takes*, however, comes with the statement that he will see what happens 'when the time comes'. He will cross the bridge when he gets there.

Father Jos watched from the sidelines as his son made this big step. Would he live up to it? There could be no excuses. He had to be a man now. This was what his father had prepared him for since infancy. The serious work had begun.

A t Catalunya on Sunday 15th May, Max Verstappen is on the second row of the grid, having qualified fourth. Two Mercedes drivers are on the front row in their Silver Arrows, Lewis Hamilton on pole position, Nico Rosberg alongside. Next to Max is new team-mate Daniel Ricciardo.

A television camera from Germany's RTL network films the Dutchman close up on the grid. He seems relaxed. His eyes look no different from normal. His left eyelid twitches a bit, but it's probably meaningless. When those cameras have to withdraw, the track is for the drivers and their cars alone.

One by one the lights go out. Revs rise, tension too. The field powers away. Verstappen loses a place to Sebastian Vettel but regains it at the third corner. Watching video footage from previous Grands Prix, Max had observed how quickly a lost position can be regained. This move, he said afterwards, was the decisive moment of his race.

Meanwhile, Hamilton makes another bad start and Rosberg shoots through the first corner in the lead. The reigning World Champion is going through a difficult period. He hasn't yet been able to win in 2016, while Rosberg has bagged all four races held so far. But Saturday's pole position has given the British driver renewed confidence, confirming that he's still capable of outpacing his hated team-mate and arch-rival. Hamilton really has to win this race because losing it would pretty much end his chances of retaining his World Championship title.

What goes on inside Hamilton's head is sometimes a mystery. Coming out of turn three, he tries to pass on the inside but Rosberg pushes him onto the grass. Hamilton loses control and gyrates into the back of his team-mate as they go into turn four. Both slide across the gravel and out of the race.

After three laps behind the safety car, the battle is wide open. Ricciardo leads from Verstappen, although the Aussie is on a different strategy. He will have to pit three times, Max only twice. And attention, of course, is also focused on the Ferraris, which are considered best of the rest.

Ricciardo is the first of the front-runners to pit. Suddenly the Dutchman is leading. The track ahead is wide open. Verstappen is like a striker sprinting towards goal. He's like the penalty taker who walks alone from the centre of the pitch to the penalty spot to take the decisive kick, watched by millions. Yet he's still only 18. An age at which you can only just vote and have a driver's licence. The tension must be unbearable. Among the spectators it certainly is. Something unprecedented is unfolding before their eyes. In the cockpit of the RB12, calmness prevails. The world may know that Max Verstappen is a cold-blooded racer, but wouldn't even an iceman melt in these circumstances?

Five laps before the end he remains self-assured. No one is going to get past him. The only uncertainty for onlookers is whether he might have to visit the pits again and trade first place for third. But his tyre management has been flawless. He continues to guide the RB12 along perfect racing lines with surgical precision, at maximum speed. Not a single mistake, nowhere a puff of smoke from wheels momentarily locking because the tyres are worn out.

For those five laps he gives Ferrari's Kimi Räikkönen, a former World Champion, a lesson in efficiency. In particular Verstappen's exit speed from the last corner, turn sixteen, makes the difference every lap. The *real* Iceman, as the Finnish fans call their idol, cannot get past. Repeatedly he falls just short of a DRS (Drag Reduction System) moment to initiate an overtaking manoeuvre.

'P1 VES'! Max and his Red Bull team celebrate in Spain, with team boss Christian Horner and team-mate Daniel Ricciardo alongside sharing his joy.

As Max takes the chequered flag, he pumps his right fist into the air in pure euphoria, but otherwise he appears to remain calm. 'If I shouted at all,' he says later, 'it was at night in my sleep, and I don't remember anything about that.'

He's so elated that every muscle in his body aches with the joy. It even makes him cramp up because he remains strapped into his car and his body can't release the tension.

When, after the slow-down lap, he parks behind the 'number 1' board and climbs out of his car, he's welcomed by Helmut Marko, the man who made the risky decision to bring him into Red Bull's first team. Politely, Max extends a hand, thanking the old man for the trust he has placed in him. It's the gesture of the student thanking the teacher. Marko won't have any of it. A handshake isn't enough to express the feeling of joy and relief. Marko embraces Max and pats him on the shoulder, then directs him towards the team. Verstappen dives into the mêlée of mechanics and does what all drivers do after a win: thank his team.

The paddock has been flipped upside-down. Photographers and camera crews are doing their best to get decent shots. They have seen this with Hamilton and Rosberg often enough but now everything is different. Here's a huge breath of fresh air.

Then comes the podium ceremony. Some people wonder if the FIA have prepared themselves for the possibility of a Dutch winner. Do they even have a recording of a national anthem that has never before been played for the winner of a Formula 1 Grand Prix? And what about the Dutch flag? That has never been displayed in the modern digital era.

Thankfully the organisers are prepared for this moment — or at least took the right steps during the race when it became clear that a driver from an unusual nation could win.

The Dutch national anthem is played, sounding somewhat tinny and unnatural through the circuit's loudspeakers. Max is dry-eyed, but his mouth quivers. He's finding it very difficult to control his emotions. His father is standing below, surrounded by media and people from the team, including Christian Horner, the boss. Jos cannot control his emotions and isn't ashamed of it.

Father and son have worked so hard for this. To achieve it, they have driven tens of thousands of miles criss-crossing Europe, from one karting track to the next. The Verstappens have put all their energy into this for years so that they could experience this precious moment, with this champagne, with this anthem.

CHAPTER 3
BEGINNINGS

Dutch sports journalist and television presenter Wilfried de Jong had the honour of introducing a very young Max Verstappen to a large audience. On 13th April 2009, Jos and his son sat in red cinema seats in the studio of the chat show *Holland Sport*. They were watching a segment in which the 11-year-old and his father were seen in their familiar surroundings — on the kart track. At that time, nobody could have foreseen how fast everything would go. Maybe only Jos himself, because it was obvious that this boy was being prepared to follow in his father's footsteps.

Max's head barely rose above the back of his seat. To his left sat the host, who, thanks to his broad interest in sport, led the conversation well. The interviewee was completely at ease and responded properly, occasionally seeking guidance from his father before coming up with his own answers.

To break the ice, they first watched a video of one of Max's kart races. This was a rare sight, because of all the sports in the Netherlands, karting gets about as much television coverage as curling — absolutely zero. Then de Jong asked his first question.

'Max, this film was shot in Genk. How many heats were there?'

Max, dressed in a neat red-and-white striped shirt, wearing a large watch on his left wrist and a microphone in his buttonhole, answered politely and firmly.

'There were four heats.'

With the next question, he already knew the answer, but the television viewer didn't.

'And how did it go?'

'I think pretty well, yes.' His eyes light up and he grins. Father Jos looks ahead sternly but cannot suppress a proud smile.

Wilfried: 'Because?'

Max, smiling a little more exuberantly: 'I won all four.'

Wilfried: 'And did you start from pole position? Because it looks like you don't have anyone in front of you.'

Max, clearly enjoying himself, smiles even more radiantly than before: 'That's right, yes.'

Wilfried: 'Great. And how old are you?'

The answer sounds forceful: 'Eleven.'

Wilfried: 'And how long have you been doing this?'

Max: 'From when I was four and a half.'

Wilfried: 'But those were smaller karts, I suppose.'

Max: 'Yes, yes.'

Wilfried: 'And did you want this yourself, or were you so proud of your father that you thought, I want that too. Say it honestly.'

Max: 'Yes, I saw others driving. They were younger than me and I thought that I want to do that too. And um... um...'

He looks aside for a moment, to see if his father might want to take over. Jos stares straight ahead, as if thinking, no, you were asked that question, son, and you have to answer it. Max speaks again, and, as if to challenge his father's silence, answers: 'At first my father didn't let me.'

The interviewer immediately picks up on this: 'Jos, what's going on here?'

It's hilarious. The backdrop on the screen is filled with smiling faces. The audience instantly falls for the charm of this amusing kid, who gazes at his father as if to say, 'Well Dad, try to get out of this one.'

Wilfried: 'Your son called you up once while you were at a Formula 1 race?'

Jos: 'My wife called me and said that he was standing by her side crying, because he wanted to drive. But I wanted to wait until he was about six, because I thought that was a good age to start. But no, he was so insistent. So I bought him a kart.

Wilfried: 'So the crying helped?'

Jos, now somewhat sterner: 'Well, I thought six was a better age. Then their understanding is a bit better and they are a bit bigger. Otherwise you have to buy a very small kart and I didn't like that. Eventually I did get it anyway.'

Two-year-old Max checks out father Jos's Arrows at the Nürburgring in 2000.

That very small kart was a toy version sold under the name Puffo, for the youngest of enthusiasts. It had a tiny motor, a tank that holds as much petrol as a cigarette lighter, and a pull-cord to start the engine. The thing didn't go fast, about 30 miles per hour at most. It was safe and cheerfully turned out, in green, yellow and red.

The interviewer takes over, turning to the type of kart he now races: 'And Max, how fast does this kart go?'

Max: 'This one goes about 100 kilometres an hour [about 60 miles per hour].'

Wilfried: 'But that's dangerous, isn't it, when I hear that speed?'

Max looks a little surprised. Danger? Come on, he never thinks about that. He wants to go fast and win. It never occurs to him that it might be dangerous.

Jos intervenes: 'Well, I always say that going to school by bike is more dangerous than what he does on the track.'

Then the conversation shifts towards the father. That he is 37 years old and has said goodbye to Formula 1, that he spends most days at the circuit in Genk working on the karts in the workshop. In fact, this is his homecoming. For him, too, it all started with karting, but not strictly with the racing. It's the preparation for racing that he finds so fascinating — the tinkering, the tuning. Endlessly working with the technology to gain speed, even if only by mere split-seconds.

He dedicates hours, days, nights even, to fiddling with mechanical minutiae on Max's karts, looking for every tenth of a second. He builds his son's karts from scratch. It all takes place at the workshop of Richard Pex, his friend in Maasbracht, where he can still be found regularly. For Verstappen Senior, tuning karts is one of the most enjoyable things there is. It's all about testing on the workbench and endlessly searching for more speed, better brakes and improved settings.

While Jos is speaking, Max looks ahead, focused and calm. He listens to stories he already knows. His posture is remarkably confident for his age. He doesn't fidget, which many other children would do. His hands rest quietly on his lap as he patiently awaits his turn. He's almost like a chess player who's mentally already four moves ahead of his opponent. This characteristic will serve him well later. People who know him and grew up with him say that Max looks far ahead. That he has answers to questions even before they're asked — which is why he finds press conferences and interviews so tedious. That he plans a passing move on the track many turns ahead.

Again the interviewer asks the right question at the right time: 'Would you be content to spend the rest of your life with your son and those karts?'

Without hesitation, Jos answers: 'Yes. I will tell you in all honesty that if he had to drive and I was in a race of my own, I would be devastated because I couldn't be with him. I've been racing since I was eight years old, but when your own child does so, you're even prouder of what he's doing than what you did yourself.'

Wilfried, turning back to Max: 'What do you learn from your father?'

Max: 'He teaches me things that I don't quite understand yet. Then he explains something and I think' — Max makes a gesture that he understands — 'oh yes, it can be done this way too.'

The interviewer continues: 'For example? How to take a corner or something?'

With the routine of a veteran, Max explains how to take a turn and then drive out of it as quickly as possible: 'From outside to inside.'

'Yes, how exactly, can you explain?'

Max answers, very seriously now: 'You brake late, steer in and then accelerate again.'

How hard can it really be? He gets excited while telling the interviewer about this technique and continues speaking, 'You do things with the carburettor and stuff.'

The interviewer isn't satisfied with that answer: 'So what do you do, adjust your set-up?'

Kart racers can adjust the carburettor while driving, to regulate the power. Jos was a phenomenon in that technique and could thus gain speed or make the engine run better if it faltered or stuttered for a moment.

Then comes the key question. The question that everyone is waiting for and that has been hanging in the air for a while. The interviewer introduces it at length to increase the tension.

A little awkwardly, Wilfried gets to the point and asks Max the question: 'Would you, after some years of karting, like to go on to Formula 1?'

Without blinking, Max says succinctly: 'Yes.'

And the strange thing is, you, the viewer, believe the kid.

So does Wilfried: 'Yes, obviously!'

Jos, laughing exuberantly: 'Indeed.'

Not long after his appearance on the television chat show *Holland Sport*, 12-year-old Max prepares for another kart race under the tutelage of father Jos.

Max wriggles in his seat for a moment in amusement.

Jos clarifies: 'It all starts in karting. He's now in his fifth season and has won 49 of the 50 races. Once he finished third, because he made a mistake on a wet part of the track. He's done all he can in the Benelux countries because he isn't yet allowed to compete with the older guys, but we're already training with them. We're really at the top and that's nice.'

Interviewer: 'So making the step to Formula 1 is a possibility?'

Jos: 'Well, I personally think we already have the plan partially ready, that he should drive karts until the age of 16 or 17 and then go into car racing.'

Interviewer: 'Are we forgetting school altogether, Jos? What kind of school is he in now?'

Max: 'Um...'

Jos: 'He's going to secondary school next year.'

Interviewer: 'Can he answer for himself, Jos?'

Jos, in a soft voice, while pointing at his son with some self-mockery, says: 'Yes, but he couldn't figure it out by himself.'

The host turns to Max again: 'Do you already know what school you want to go to?'

The youngster really has to think hard now. School? You can see in his eyes that he's thinking... School? But I don't have time for that, do I? I want to be a Formula 1 driver. You don't learn that at school.

Jos intervenes as a responsible parent: 'We have an appointment with the headteacher. Next year we will have to go abroad for a few weeks: Germany, Italy, France. He'll get time off if his grades are good. I think that's important. If they're not, he won't get any time off.'

The interviewer continues: 'You and your father are next to each other on an empty track. And I'm waving the flag for the start. You start right next to each other: who is going to win?'

Max looks at Wilfried intently while listening to that question. He promptly answers: 'That's hard to say.'

The interviewer reacts surprised: 'Difficult to say, difficult to say, do you know who you're talking to? Your father! A Formula 1 driver who twice finished third in a Grand Prix. You can't beat that, can you? Come on, you're only 11!'

Max explains: 'We never drive the same kart.'

Wilfried: 'So there's a chance you could beat your father?'

Max: 'There is that chance.'

CHAPTER 3

When Max was born, on 30th September 1997 in Hasselt, Belgium, Jos was a celebrated Formula 1 driver, but Max's mother, Sophie Kumpen, had also enjoyed success in karting. She became Belgian champion twice and regularly made it onto the podium in various international competitions. She raced against renowned drivers such as Jenson Button, Giancarlo Fisichella and Jarno Trulli, all of whom she regularly beat. Sometimes she also beat Jos.

People who have seen Max grow up say that he has the genes of both his father and his mother. In Max's case, though, one plus one equals three. He also has his mother's charm and his father's fighting spirit.

'Under that helmet he's a tiger,' his mother says. In the same vein, she adds, 'Max never used to play the boss at home, he left that to his sister. He always gave her the sticker book or colouring book to keep the peace. He always thinks of her. They're really close. It's his character: kind and sweet. Max will always want to solve things by talking first, he's the feeling type. That fierceness, and racing, he gets that from Jos. The gentle part comes more from me.'

Max grew up with his father in Maaseik, a stone's throw from the circuit in Genk and close to their workshop in Maasbracht. This was agreed when his parents divorced. That ended a turbulent period, with many arguments. Latterly, when the family had gone on holiday, the parents had slept separately with a child each, Max in Jos's room, sister Victoria with Sophie. And that's how the divorce was arranged. Max moved in with Jos, Victoria stayed with Sophie. The young boy's future was in his father's hands. He would become a racing driver.

Racing against friends inside a local warehouse, first with a pedal kart, then a quad bike, became Max's favourite pastime, in addition to regular visits to the kart track at Genk. Every free Wednesday, Saturday and Sunday, Max went to the Genk track with his father, who in turn had spent lots of time there as a youth. Holidays were planned around karting events in Germany, Italy and France. Max raced with peers, but especially learned a great deal from competing against older friends. One of them was Jorrit Pex, two years older and 2015 karting world champion. Max was regularly the best. And convincingly so, such that his kart was often checked by the stewards because there was a suspicion that he had a stronger engine than allowed. Later, this also happened regularly in Formula 3, where his car would be stripped down to the last bolt to see if there was any hidden advantage. There never was. In

Max's mother, Sophie, was a successful racer herself.

Max's karts, it was Jos's commitment that provided the extra power and the driver's skill that made the best use of it.

Some sceptics have claimed that Max is Jos 2.0, a copy of his father. That's only partly true. Although Jos carefully protected his son, Max developed in his own way in his younger years. He was always his own man. His former team boss in Formula 3, Frits van Amersfoort, says: 'Jos arranged it all and gave advice, but Max absorbed everything like a sponge and made his own decisions where necessary.'

Dennis van de Laar, Max's team-mate in Florida in 2014, says: 'There can be seven Josses at the side of the track, but ultimately there's only one Max in the cockpit and he has to make the decisions.'

Yet Jos's firm hand did have an undeniable impact on the youngster. Max's upbringing by his father was so exceptionally firm and focused that some loving parents might judge it to have been potentially damaging. Will Buxton hesitantly reflects on this: 'It's a very strange relationship. Max and Jos have been very open about it, always. Max would tell how angry his father could be with him if he hadn't done well. There's a story about how Jos dropped him off somewhere in the south of France and then drove away... Is that tough love, or is it damaging to a child when the relationship is that extreme? I will in no way question the love Max feels for his father. But as a father, it's a big risk to put so much pressure on your child.'

Parenting is balancing on a tightrope, Buxton underlines: 'If Max expressed the wish to become a Formula 1 driver, Jos had to show him tough love. To build up his character and give him a thick skin in preparation for his arrival. Jos knows how terrible that Formula 1 world is. It takes no prisoners: it can chew people up, spit them out and never think of them again. Jos did have to toughen him up to prepare him for it... Max tells those stories now, as if it did nothing to him, only made him stronger. But others might look and think: God, this is terrible, how can a parent do this to their child? But hey, this is how it worked between Max and Jos. To get him where he is, it was necessary. And now? Max adores his father, the two have a great relationship.'

In Sarno, southern Italy, the 14-year-old was in outstanding form on his way to the 125cc KZ2 karting world title of 2013. He qualified fastest and dominated the pre-final. In the final, he started from pole, but lost a place immediately after the start — a rare occurrence. On the second lap he tried to regain the lost ground with an out-of-character kamikaze move. The resulting crash damaged the kart so badly that he couldn't continue.

Verstappen Senior, who had prepared the kart with the dedication of a craftsman and a father, was furious. Junior had ignored his teaching. Most fathers would offer a comforting shoulder, or simply shrug and say, 'Better luck next time, son.' But there was no sympathy. An icy silence ensued. While Max admitted his error and, with tears in his eyes, asked his father if the damaged kart should be loaded into the van for the long journey home, he was told to go and collect it himself. So Max did, with someone's help. Meanwhile, Max tried to reduce the tension by starting a conversation, but his father wouldn't have it. 'Don't talk to me,' he said bitterly. 'You've ruined the race and I'm sick to death of it.'

Jos had spent weeks preparing the kart for this race and all the work had been undone by a basic mistake. It was the sort of error he no longer expected from his son, who by now had to know what he could and couldn't do. He considered the overtaking attempt unworthy of Max. Now, looking back at this incident, the basis of Max's ability to stay out of trouble at the start of a Formula 1 race, to get through the first corners damage-free, surely lies in the impeccable style he developed when karting.

For seven days Jos didn't speak to his son. In *De Telegraaf*, the leading Dutch newspaper, Jos recalled the experience: 'I was really pissed off and I wanted to hit him where it hurt.' After a week of silence, the matter was set aside and normality resumed. Later Max would acknowledge that he learned a lot from the Sarno incident and would never make such a mistake again. Jos also has no regrets whatsoever about his harsh reaction. In the documentary *Whatever It Takes*, he says that the incident may have been a crucial moment in his son's development. Never again would Max make an error like that, he felt sure.

Jos's commitment to turn his son into a racing superstar borders on the unfathomable. Together they drove over 100,000 miles around Europe in an exercise that's estimated to have cost at least £500,000. At one time, they were returning from a race in southern Germany when rain suddenly started to fall. They immediately turned round in order to get in a few more practice sessions on a wet track.

It was rarely necessary to correct, motivate or pressure the boy. His father's lessons in all sorts of areas — from codes of conduct in the paddock to driving technique — fell on fertile ground. Even at the hated press conferences after races and practice sessions, where many journalists ask 'extremely stupid and always the same' questions in the eyes of father and son, Max conducts himself 'flawlessly' in Jos's eyes. The motto is just to be direct and that's exactly what he has learned to do.

Max's karting past is often left unmentioned by the media, because karting is a branch of motorsport that takes place largely outside the spotlight and is all but unknown to the general public. Even motocross gets more attention in the media. But in his run-up to the big league, the youngster's performance was nothing short of astounding. He usually won, often from pole position because he was virtually unbeatable in qualifying. The rest of the field was often left far behind.

Paul Lemmens, owner of the kart track in Genk, said of him: 'He drove off and nobody saw him again. It was unbelievable, the way that boy can race. I've only seen that with the all-time greats, like Jenson Button and Fernando Alonso.'

The trophy cabinet soon filled up. Not even other karting stars who reached Formula 1 — names like Ayrton Senna, Michael Schumacher and Jenson Button — could match his record. Furthermore, none of them started so early: Senna entered his first kart race at 13, Schumacher at 12, and Button (also partly trained in Genk) at eight.

Besides Max's incredible talent, his karts were special because they were built and prepared by his father. The same could be said of Senna, but his father only made his first kart, based on a lawnmower engine. Max's equipment was put together by his father throughout his karting career and was spot-on from day one.

Max's first race came at the age of seven, in the north-eastern Dutch town of Emmen in April 2003. That's when his father immediately saw that his boy had talent. The little lad sat there on the front row surrounded by 18 older boys aged between 10 and 12. He sped off and none of his rivals saw him again. His father stood there in awe and admiration, watching Max win his very first race with ease. It was a watershed moment, even if the youngster could still choose a football career.

In 2005, he took part in the Belgian championship in the mini class, winning all 21 races, and after that he continued to win everything. In 2013, he graduated from his junior career with a world KZ championship title in Varennes-sur-Allier, France.

He has never been afraid of speed, but then speed isn't necessarily something to be afraid of. Cycling is more dangerous than motor racing; even football

Besides his own prodigious talent, Max benefited from his father's immaculate preparation of his karts.

has fatalities through heart failure. The thought of 200 miles per hour in a Formula 1 car may seem an incredible speed, and it is, but in karts the perceived speed is just as high. With a 125cc engine, six gears, 42 horsepower and weight of about 90 kilograms, a kart may be a fairly simple machine, but its top speed of roughly 85 miles per hour is comparable with that of a Formula 1 car when scale is taken into account. Speed can also feel more intense in a kart because the driver sits so close to the ground and can get through corners so quickly because stiff suspension, grippy tyres and a low centre of gravity provide amazing road-holding characteristics. A kart almost literally sticks to the tarmac. Experts say that Max 'drives with his butt', something he learned in karting, along with cornering techniques and finding the ideal racing lines.

The only person who sometimes got scared was his mother Sophie. On one occasion when he was very young she saw him go off the track. She ran to the scene, in high heels and short denim skirt, almost crying with concern. But Max was already retrieving his kart and getting back in. 'Nothing's wrong, Mum.'

By the end of 2013 there was nothing left to win. Karting was done. He had outgrown that arena and was ready for a new adventure.

But he was still only 15, an age when it's easy to get lost in a plethora of different racing categories without proper guidance. Mercedes team principal Toto Wolff wanted him, but he would only have been eligible to race in the *Deutsche Tourenwagen Meisterschaft* (DTM), Germany's prestigious touring car championship, because the Formula 1 team didn't have a suitable training programme in place. But with Jos there to guide him, there was no chance that Max could lose his way, even if a significant extra factor now came into play — money.

In so many other sports — football, tennis, gymnastics, athletics — it's all about a pair of shoes, the right clothing, a few bits of equipment and travel expenses. In motor racing you need a fast car and a team to run it. A year in the GP2 series, one of the gateways to Formula 1, can cost as much as £1 million. Drivers invariably have to buy their seats and can do so through sponsorship money but finding that money is far from easy. Even karting champions who have the potential to become world champions don't get a free seat.

Matching money to the talent was the task that now faced Team Verstappen. They weighed up the various options. There was always the fear that a wrong

Max's final year of karting, 2013, delivered his world championship title driving this 125cc CRG kart.

choice could seriously impede Max's progress, even though insiders were certain that his talent would shine through regardless.

The young Max was improbably fast, hardly ever made a mistake and won everything. Much the same is true of the slightly older Max. Everything in the boy from the outset seemed destined for racing — and for winning. His attitude, his work ethic and his eagerness to learn were unsurpassable.

CHAPTER 4
JOS

Without Jos, no Max. That's logical, isn't it? Jos Verstappen was the most successful Dutch Formula 1 driver of all time until 2016. A driver who perhaps didn't, or couldn't, get the most out of his career. That often happens in motor racing, where talent isn't only the factor in achieving success.

Many fans believe that Jos had it in him to be World Champion, had he been in the right car. Other observers claim that fate always determines where you end up. No hard evidence can be found to support either position.

Jos's career also began with the magic of the go-kart and the smell of motor oil. He did it all himself and even used to fit the tyres to his own kart at the track in Genk, which in the 1980s was much the same as it is now.

The world of motorsport, however, looked very different back then. In Jos's early years, there was hardly any motorsport in his home province of Limburg. No circuit, no drivers. Dutch racing drivers at that time came mainly from the west, near Zandvoort, the country's most important racetrack. Limburg, the southernmost of the 12 provinces in the Netherlands, was distant and different, a landscape of rolling countryside, an area traditionally known for coal mining and carnivals. Limburgers felt little attachment to the Randstad, the densely populated and affluent conurbation of the western Netherlands, even though it was only a hundred miles away.

Then suddenly a racer from the south appeared who gave the western part of the country 'a run for its money'. A guy with enormous commitment and

Like Max, Jos Verstappen drove for Van Amersfoort Racing, winning the
German Formula 3 Championship in 1993 with sponsorship from
Philips, the Dutch electronics giant.

passion — and a goal. His aim was to reach Formula 1 and win there. That was quite a job for a kid who grew up in a mobile home.

This ambitious newcomer had to pay for all his expensive equipment himself. In the Netherlands, even tennis was still considered an elite sport in those days. Golf was only played on private courses, for which high fees had to be paid. The Netherlands may have been prosperous, but that prosperity had clear limits. Football was far and away the country's most popular sport. As for motor racing, that was left trailing because of lack of success, facilities and infrastructure. Aspiring Dutch racing drivers had to figure it out for themselves.

And then there's the sheer cost of climbing the ladder in motorsport. There was no way that Jos's family could help him. Grandfather Sjef had a scrapyard, father Frans a café called De Rotonde (The Roundabout). Later Jos himself opened a go-kart workshop on the other side of the street from the café. These Verstappens were ordinary, hard-working people, without pretensions. Their world consisted of Montfort and the surrounding area.

Jos was left to his own devices. If he wanted to achieve something in motor racing, he had to do it all himself. Tinkering, tuning, racing, travelling — all while also having to earn a living. He had to make it happen with his talent, inventiveness, perseverance and enthusiasm.

Just as Max has Jos's genes, Jos has the genes of his father, Frans, who was known as hard and uncompromising. The Verstappens know no middle ground. It's all or nothing. If Jos did something wrong, he was sometimes locked in the family's modest home for hours on end. Crying didn't help and neither did the conciliatory words of his mother. Sister Gerda told the daily newspaper *De Volkskrant*: 'Father would have these fits. If he had a fight with Jos they would almost bash each other's brains in. For my mother this bickering was difficult. She has a gentle character and always protected Jos. But my father thought that as his wife she should choose his side.'

Jos could often be found at his grandfather's scrapyard, riding dirt bikes. He also busied himself with the wrecked cars, learning and fettling.

When Jos started karting, he picked it up quickly and soon made a name for himself as a promising talent. He won his first major race at the age of 12, in 1984, and went on to become that year's Dutch junior champion. Two European karting titles followed.

In his youth, he was just as eager to learn as Max. To be able to do more karting, he decided to work at the karting track in Genk, about 30 miles south-west of his home town, across the border in Belgium. While he based himself there, owner Paul Lemmens allowed him to use the track and the facilities. What Jos didn't know, he wanted to learn.

Jos made the transition from karting to proper single-seater racing for the 1992 season and seemed unstoppable. As a rookie driver in Frits van Amersfoort's team, he spent that year in Formula Opel Lotus, a strong single-seater category at the time, and won 11 races from 18 starts, enough to make him Benelux champion. This 'one-make' series, based upon the same type of Reynard car, was an objective measure of a driver's qualities because everyone had equal equipment.

Van Amersfoort remembers in particular Jos's international début at Zolder: 'He was unbeatable. It seemed as if he had more horsepower than the rest. Zolder is a real steering circuit, where it doesn't come down to straight-line speed, and that's when the Verstappens are at their best. You can see that with Max as well. These are guys who grew up with karts, who can steer like a jazz musician can play the piano blind. I'm a fan of Dave Brubeck, a virtuoso who played completely by feeling. The Verstappens can do that with a car.'

Jos stayed with van Amersfoort for 1993, moving up to Formula 3. He won the prestigious Masters of Formula 3 event at Zandvoort, the year's biggest fixture in the category, and also widened his horizons by competing in the German Formula 3 Championship and winning that too.

The expression 'death or glory' certainly applied to Jos's driving style as well as his career. As van Amersfoort says: 'With Jos, it's black or white. With him around, there's always something happening. He's a stirrer. He isn't a difficult character, but he's extreme, in a lot of things. If he couldn't pass someone on the track, he might go over them if necessary. As a result, he has done many good things, but sometimes he has also done stupid things. That's the tragedy of Jos.'

His attacking style appealed to the public. He represented an approach to sport that had been epitomised by the Dutch football team for a wonderful but short-lived period in the 1970s. During the 1974 World Cup, when the Netherlands reached the final only to lose to West Germany, the national team was hailed for its adventurous and exciting style, which became an example for the rest of the world to follow. Four years later, the Netherlands again made it to the final, this time against Argentina, but now the fire in the team's game had been extinguished.

Looked at in this context, it isn't surprising that an individualistic character like Jos Verstappen was embraced so strongly by his country's motorsport fans. His assertive, combative, uncompromising racing style was in tune with the national character, just as it is with Max now. Before long, a huge fan club developed, and the small town of Montfort — with the café and the karting centre — became a destination of pilgrimage for his followers. Fans even came just to touch the wall of the café.

In truth, Jos became too casual about his popularity. For him, racing was racing. Nothing more and nothing less. The charade around it was just a burden. He could be himself on the track, in the car, in the race. People who tried to polish his image were left disappointed. This racing driver, who could be ill-humoured and undiplomatic, didn't want a brand identity. The website, built by diehard fans, was enough for him.

He wanted to tell his story on the racetrack. The rest was just noise. It's no surprise that his first season in Formula 1 was both spectacular and tarnished.

Jos started in a top team. It happened more or less by chance. When Benetton's Flavio Briatore signed him, the intention was that he would spend his first year, 1994, as reserve and test driver, playing a supporting role to Michael Schumacher and JJ Lehto. Fate decided otherwise. When Lehto got injured in pre-season testing, 22-year-old Jos was pushed through to the starting grid. Suddenly there he was at the first race of the season amidst all the Formula 1 aces, including Ayrton Senna, Damon Hill, Jean Alesi — and his illustrious team leader.

With hindsight, it's easy to judge that the young Jos Verstappen entered the game too soon, that he should have waited a year. He later admitted as much.

There were doubts in the Verstappen camp. His manager, Huub Rothengatter, called his friend Kees van de Grint beforehand to ask for advice. Was it wise? Should a young driver really get on this express train at this early stage of a career? Van de Grint said, 'Why not? I don't believe in learning years. The really great talents are right there. A learning year is a lost year in my view. And if you don't get on the train, you never know when the next one will come along.'

Jos and Rothengatter decided that he would jump onboard. Jos stepped into the blue-green Benetton-Ford B194 to make his Formula 1 début in the Brazilian Grand Prix on 27th March 1994. This was a racing team with sky-high expectations. The pressure was on right away. Maybe not immediately from the outside world, but certainly from within himself.

I f Jos Verstappen was the director of his movie, then Huub Rothengatter was the producer. Huub was the deal maker. He was the instigator, catalyst and mentor behind Jos Verstappen the racing driver.

Rothengatter arranged everything for years. He was the first to recognise Jos as an uncut diamond. 'Raw Talent' was the slogan with which the driver was presented at the 1993 Marlboro Masters of Formula 3 event at Zandvoort. Jos won it. With that, he put his money where his mouth was. Rothengatter introduced him to the market, so to speak, and Verstappen Senior lived up to expectations. The 'Masters' was an ideal showcase and later winners included Lewis Hamilton, Nico Hülkenberg, Valtteri Bottas — and Max Verstappen. It was the first time the general public in the Netherlands became acquainted with a new phenomenon. With that victory in the 'Masters', the catchy slogan, 'Raw Talent, True Passion', as it fully read, gained enough credibility to kickstart his racing career. Rothengatter opened doors that remained closed for others.

It's too much to conclude that Jos Verstappen was the product of Huub Rothengatter, but it was close. Without this shrewd manager and businessman, he might never have ended up in Formula 1.

Rothengatter's role in Max Verstappen's story also shouldn't be underestimated. Huub was there for Jos and he was there for Max. He pulled the decisive strings when necessary and believed in Max so much that he fully financed his seat in Formula 3 with Frits van Amersfoort. In his eyes, there was no doubt. Max was going to be Formula 1 World Champion and he wanted to contribute to that.

Formula 1 is a world of networking and Rothengatter could do that better than anyone. In this motorsport business worth billions, it's by no means certain that the greatest talents behind the wheel actually end up in the premier league. Ayrton Senna once said, 'Maybe the greatest racing talent is driving around as a forklift driver in Mumbai.' The less competitive teams are only too happy to hire paying drivers to make ends meet. Rather that, than a driver who might be better, but brings no money. Sometimes it seems to be a sport that has become too expensive to accommodate its brilliance.

Until 2014, Huub Rothengatter was a constant factor in the story of the Verstappens — and to a degree the story of Dutch motorsport too. His name has popped up in various places over the years but nevertheless a somewhat mysterious aura surrounds him. He rarely gives interviews, because, as he says himself, he always tells the truth and might therefore antagonise people. He appears to cherish his place in the shadows.

As with Max, Huub Rothengatter played a big part in Jos Verstappen's career, as manager, sponsorship-getter and friend.

How Huub played an important role on Max's path to Formula 1 is for others to tell. One element in that role is that Max's current manager, Raymond Vermeulen, is a Rothengatter protégé. But Huub himself doesn't want to share anything about it. Even at the beginning of 2016, when everything suddenly changed and Max Verstappen stepped up to the Red Bull team, he didn't want to speak about his part in the story. He had moved on with his life.

Rothengatter used to be a Formula 1 driver. He drove with Ayrton Senna in the last Dutch Grand Prix of the old era, at Zandvoort in 1985. They shared the same track, but that's all. Rothengatter was uncompetitive in his Alfa Romeo-powered Osella and wasn't classified as a finisher, whereas Senna finished third in his Lotus-Renault. Huub didn't have that much driving talent, but he did have enormous perseverance and entrepreneurial creativity. He himself was the first to put his qualities as a racing driver into perspective: 'Well, racing is a bit of an overstatement in my case; I chased the field ahead of me.'

As a driver, Rothengatter followed the usual route to Formula 1. After Formula Ford, he went into Formula 2, and remained the only Dutchman to have won a Formula 2 race — at Zolder in 1980 — until Richard Verschoor emulated his feat in 2021. For the 1984 season, he secured a Formula 1 seat as a paying driver at the Spirit team, following that with further Formula 1 rides with Osella in 1985 and Zakspeed in 1986. The inimitable way in which he managed to secure sponsorship even drew international attention and nowadays the English-language Wikipedia entry for him mentions that his greatest achievement has been his ability to attract personal sponsors.

For example, in the mid-1980s he bought two pages in *De Telegraaf*, then the largest newspaper in the Netherlands, with more than a million copies sold daily. With the headline 'Interested Mr. Philips?' and a manipulated photo of a racing car covered with the name of the famous Dutch manufacturer of electrical goods, he managed to draw attention to himself. The campaign was accompanied by eye-catching phrases such as 'One billion viewers worldwide, thirty drivers at the start' and 'The desire to drive at the front of one billion viewers in a Philips car is very great'.

The advertisement cost 70,000 guilders — about £18,000 at the time. Although it didn't bring in a major sponsor, Eindhoven-based Philips was so charmed by the initiative that the company spontaneously reimbursed the cost. Later, Rothengatter became a promoter for Philips's motorsport involvement, and the company became a sponsor of... Jos Verstappen.

After a conflict just before Max arrived at the doorstep of Formula 1, the

Racing with Benetton in 1994, Jos found himself overshadowed as team leader Michael Schumacher drove imperiously to the first of his seven World Championship titles.

An infamous moment in Jos's first year of Formula 1 came when spilled fuel ignited during a pitstop in the German Grand Prix at Hockenheim.

long and fruitful Rothengatter/Verstappen collaboration came to an end. 'Huub is Huub and Jos is Jos,' says Frits van Amersfoort.

Back to Jos Verstappen's début at Interlagos in 1994. It was an unfortunate race, a portent for the rest of the season. Through no fault of his own, Jos collided with Jordan driver Eddie Irvine and became involved in one of that year's biggest crashes. Irvine was suspended for three races and Jos got noticed, although not necessarily in a good way. But even if he was innocent, a crash in the first race is never recommended and it put an immediate blemish on his record.

Jos wasn't used to playing second fiddle. He had been the best in every category until he reached Formula 1. His character didn't allow losing and yet he couldn't help but lose, because with Michael Schumacher as his team-mate he could never win. In that memorable first race of 1994, which Schumacher won, the German driver even held off Ayrton Senna, who would so tragically perish at Imola just five weeks later.

Verstappen Senior's year at Benetton seemed like an all-action movie, full of heroism and tragedy. It was clearly a great contrast to the arrival of his 17-year-old son in 2015. Compared with the wild storm that enveloped his father, Max sailed across ripple-free seas.

Jos's début season turned out to be a thriller. It had everything: fierce battles, hard-earned podium finishes, a pit fire, political manoeuvring by the team's leadership, and a monumental crash. He was the David who didn't shy away from taking the fight to Goliath. In this case, team-mate Schumacher. And because in love and war anything is allowed, Jos also employed strategic means when it served his purposes. If one thing sets the Verstappens apart from everything and everyone else, it's the will to win.

After just two races Jos was pushed aside, in favour of the recovered JJ Lehto. Five races later he returned, because Lehto hadn't performed well enough. But at the end of the season, the Dutchman had to give way again, this time for the more experienced Johnny Herbert.

This was the year Jos told the media that there was a button on Schumacher's steering wheel but he didn't know what it was for. This was the year Benetton was accused of equipping Schumacher with traction control, which was banned, because he always got away so well at the start. Could that button have been for that purpose? There was wild speculation in the media, conspiracy theories indeed, like a movie script. Why did Verstappen say what he said? What did he want to achieve? Was it even true? Was saying it stupid or smart?

But perhaps Jos was still too inexperienced to really understand the politics of Formula 1. Whatever, he became good friends with his German team leader. The Schumacher and Verstappen families spent time with each other and even went on skiing holidays together.

Jos also nearly lost his life with Benetton. The pit fire at Hockenheim in 1994 is one of the most famous moments in Formula 1 history. Somehow he miraculously escaped with only minor burns.

Between all the incidents, the 22-year-old Verstappen tried to hold his own, but his performances over the season — his best results were third places in Hungary and Belgium — were insufficient to convince the team bosses to keep him. Or was there more at play? Was it known by now that Team Verstappen negotiated hard and proved to be a difficult business partner in the commercial arena? In any case, what was supposed to be a triumphant trip to the top with Benetton became, in the years that followed, an inglorious tour with backmarkers, in which there was no honour to be gained, not even for a driver as good as him.

Frits van Amersfoort: 'Jos always went pedal to the metal. There was no middle ground. He had to be the best, even if he couldn't be. But that's his instinct and that's also his great strength. Still. If Max doesn't win, or things work against him, Jos throws the headphones off his head. I think that's beautiful. Emotion is part of top sport. Jos was like that during his racing career. I wasn't present, but I think at Benetton there was a storm from time to time.'

In that extreme year in the Benetton team, his inexperience and his character, as well as the part played by politics, prevented him from achieving his great ambition: to win a Grand Prix.

'It was a different time,' Jos later acknowledged with a calmness that's at odds with his racing temperament. 'I still had to figure everything out by myself.'

Formula 1 has evolved since then. These days it's a tightly managed show, where pitstop fires are out of the question and speed in the pitlane has been curbed. It's all more rigidly controlled, written to the beat of a new generation of drivers who have grown up in a virtual world.

The views of fellow Dutch racer Jan Lammers are instructive: 'Jos was like an electric motor as a driver. When switched on, he reached pole speed straight away. It was impressive. His performance was immediately explosive. He was always in the spotlight. The downside was that when he started like that, the expectations for the weekend suddenly became sky-high. But he had started at such a high level that sometimes the progression wasn't there anymore.

'The first thing that struck me about Max, besides him being fast, is that he builds up in such a calm and calculated way. That's no coincidence. He inherited that from his mother, who can also be very calm. Max has the explosiveness of his father and the poise of his mother. He can keep his head down and evolve over a weekend. Just look at how he did at his first race in the Red Bull in Spain. In a new car, anticipating his chance and striking. You saw that happen in the 2015 season as well. When it was needed, he was there. Moreover, he showed progression throughout the year.

'Jos went like hell, but also over the limit at times. Max is different.'

Although Jos lost his Formula 1 seat to Johnny Herbert at the end of 1994, he remained under contract with Benetton for a second year and Flavio Briatore loaned him to the Simtek team, only for that to turn sour when Simtek went bust after just five races. Gloomy spells followed with Footwork Arrows (1996), Tyrrell (1997) and Stewart (1998).

Then a great new opportunity arose when Honda decided to enter Formula 1 with Jos as number one driver. The Japanese manufacturer's team would be built around him and chief engineer Harvey Postlethwaite. Verstappen, now aged 26, was in the prime of his life. Postlethwaite was an experienced and highly regarded British designer who had enjoyed a six-year spell at Ferrari during which his turbocharged 126C2 had twice won the Formula 1 constructors' championship. It seemed that the Dutchman was finally back at a team with the potential to reach the top.

But fate intervened when Postlethwaite died of a heart attack during an early-season test in Barcelona. Honda pulled the plug, leaving Jos without a drive in 1999. It was a lost year. Two seasons followed with Arrows and then a final year of Formula 1 with Minardi.

'I have great admiration for Jos,' says Kees van de Grint, 'because he just kept on going. I hate flying long distances and I think Jos must have felt that too. But for Jos it was worse. He flew 21 hours to Australia knowing he could never win. And he kept that up for ten years, while I knew there was a winner in him. That must have been extremely frustrating for him. But still he kept at it and saw light at the end of the tunnel, however small.'

The few opportunities to shine usually came as a result of calamities or changing weather conditions, when horsepower matters less. These rare occasions allowed him to show how fast he really was. In 2000, driving for Arrows, he had such a peak. He managed to finish fifth in Canada with a car that should have been at the back. If he ever gave a demonstration of sheer determination, it was in this wet race.

A year later in Malaysia he was just as impressive. It was an exceptional performance that moved Michael Schumacher to say 'Jos was flying'. In pouring rain, he climbed from 18th to sixth place within one lap, overtaking, among others, Jenson Button, Giancarlo Fisichella, Kimi Räikkönen, Jean Alesi, Eddie Irvine, Nick Heidfeld and Olivier Panis. Moments later he was second, right behind David Coulthard's McLaren. He fought superb duels with Ralf Schumacher (Williams) and Mika Häkkinen (McLaren). Towards the end, a pitstop dropped him from fourth to seventh, which is where he finished. Afterwards, he said proudly, 'Give me a top car and I'll make it hard for the big boys every time.'

That top car never came. That was reserved for Max, many years later.

By 2003 Jos's Formula 1 career was over. Max was six at the time. Everyone knew Jos could drive like a devil, but also that he went over the limit too often. That earned him the unflattering nickname 'Jos Grindbak' — meaning 'Gravel Bucket'.

His talent was widely recognised among experts and knowledgeable fans. For the general public, though, it all diminished as he slipped further and further down the field.

Jos became a cult hero in the Netherlands. His fan base was larger than the fan clubs of some professional football clubs. When the Internet began to take off, the website *verstappen.nl* became one of the busiest in the Netherlands. It has since evolved into a meeting place and information source for Max's fans.

Although Jos disappeared from Formula 1, his driving career didn't quite finish. He competed in the 2005–06 A1 Championship for Team Netherlands, run by Jan Lammers. Into 2008 he raced in the Le Mans Series, a haven for many ex-single-seater drivers. Twice he took part in the Le Mans 24 Hours, finishing 10th in 2008 in a Dutch-entered Porsche and 13th in 2009 for the factory Aston Martin team.

But by this time he was deeply involved in something else. He had returned to his roots, karting, with a young lad called Max, a name chosen not entirely accidentally. This was to be Jos's new destiny.

Even in the later stages of his career driving for uncompetitive teams, Jos produced flashes of brilliance. One such occasion was at the Canadian Grand Prix of 2000 when he brought his Arrows home in fifth place. Besides having an Orange-sponsored car, for this race Jos adopted an orange helmet to show his support for the Dutch national football team at Euro 2000.

CHAPTER 5
TRACK OF CHAMPIONS

The track gleams in the spring sunshine. Like a snake, its 1,400 metres of tarmac wind through a grassy expanse. This is the track of champions. This is where Max Verstappen first tasted motorsport, as a four-year-old boy who wanted to race a go-kart, because his younger friend was allowed to. With tears in his eyes, he asked his father if he could have a go-kart as well. The father was strict. This was out of the question. He was still too young. He needed to wait a few more years — an answer the boy didn't want to hear.

It was no coincidence that young Max was at Genk that day. This karting track is a thread that's woven through the life of the Verstappens. Jos was always at home here — and still is. Even now, Max likes to drive here in his spare time.

'Karting is a bit like Formula 1,' says track owner Paul Lemmens, 'but without budgets of millions and strict rules — and it takes place away from the eyes of the media. The sport is still a hobby for the great drivers. They love to do it. It's the rock 'n' roll of motorsport.'

Genk is a legend among devotees. World-famous racers can lap Europe's longest outdoor kart circuit in anonymity. Wearing an ordinary integral helmet and an unidentified racesuit removes them from the fame that can be oppressive.

'They can be themselves here,' says Lemmens, although he's quick to add that the drivers who return here from time to time don't act like prima donnas. 'You should understand that racing is a very democratic sport.'

We're in the circuit's café. It's ordinary, almost like a café at a small football club, except that the view from it isn't of a pitch but of a karting track. The building is located alongside the track, right next to the podium where prizes are awarded after the various races, with the traditional chequered flag as the backdrop. A large terrace in front of the café offers a good view of the racing action. The tables on the terrace are shaped like Red Bull cans.

Genk is a public facility. Ordinary karts with four-stroke engines are available for hire and for tuition, but they still achieve impressive top speeds. This is why the track is so popular for company outings and groups of friends who want to have fun for an afternoon. It does seem to be a man's world. The whole place, in fact, seems to have the allure of a football club. At the entrance there's a banner with the slogan 'From karting in Genk to F1'. It has pictures of drivers who made it, big names, including Michael Schumacher. There's also a picture of little Max Verstappen with big Jenson Button, who crouched when it was taken so that their heads are level. And a photo of father Jos, just before the start of a race, with long-legged girls carrying parasols in the background — this is motorsport after all.

Formula 1's glitzy paddock is light years away from this simple world. Here, speed is generated by small engines, the café is for simple refreshment and socialising, and no million-dollar deals are made. Sponsors are few and far between. Keeping a kart team on the track is a hobby that doesn't earn a penny.

'You should be happy if you can just get some of your equipment sponsored,' says Lemmens, raising his voice slightly. Not out of anger, but emotion. Elderly though he is, with reading glasses hanging folded over his striped shirt, his enthusiasm remains evident when it comes to motorsport. He still works every day at the track, where the stars of the past sometimes drop by. He's in regular contact with Jenson Button, his favourite protégé, with whom he chats or messages at least once a month. He hasn't spotted any new superstars for a while. For the time being, thinks Lemmens, Max is the most recent one: 'It will take some time before another talent of that level emerges.'

He's nothing like the suave principal of a Formula 1 team. On the contrary. He's the manager of a racetrack who regularly rides his bicycle around it to check everything. It seems to be quite hard work running this place. 'But,' says Lemmens, his eyes sparkling, 'it's also a hobby, and I happened to be able to make a living out of it.'

Here, at the bottom layer of motorsport, there's no pot of gold to be found.

This is where the foundations of the sport are built, purely through talent and hard work. It's work that needs to be done every day. Loading the trailers, keeping the organisation running, sweeping the track, restocking. 'If I can't do it myself, I won't come here anymore.'

Referring back to an earlier part of the conversation, I ask Lemmens what he means about the democratic aspect of motorsport.

'Well, people sometimes think that motor racing is an elite sport, but nothing could be further from the truth. All the boys I've seen over the years have come from humble backgrounds. Sons of ordinary families, not particularly rich. They had to work very hard to get to where they are now and did everything they could to get there. Take Jos as an example. He was obsessed with the sport. Unbelievably obsessed, a perfectionist. He was always trying to win something. In his lap times, in his technique. He never gave up and above all he was very talented. When you work with someone like that, it's very nice. You always get something in return. He wasn't rich. He had to do everything himself. But none of the guys who drove here were rich.

'Nor were other drivers like Fernando Alonso, Jarno Trulli and Giancarlo Fisichella. They drove fast, but none of them were millionaires. Motor racing is an expensive business and it becomes more expensive the further you get. So every driver needs sponsors and that's where the money comes from — not from the boys themselves. Jos had to help here with all kinds of things, because he wanted to use the track. Jenson didn't have millions either. With Jos and Jenson, as well as everybody in Formula 1, their real driving talent has been appreciated.'

While we're talking, Lemmens frequently takes a sweet from a tray on the table in front of us. He puts one after another in his mouth.

The stout Belgian has been in karting for a lifetime. He started when races were simply held on public roads. He mentions the town of Hoensbroek, just across the border in the Netherlands, where karts used to race round the streets, much as cyclists do. He talks about big crowds turning out to watch those events long ago and remembers a figure of 7,000 people.

'Today, people around here seem to be increasingly negative,' he continues. 'If the wind takes the sound in the wrong direction, there's always someone on the phone complaining. If the grass is being cut here, the police are called. Just think: over the years we have already reduced noise by 16 decibels! You know what a difference just one decibel makes?

Paul Lemmens — the man behind the illustrious kart track at Genk.

'Is that why there are so few international drivers in the Netherlands? The Netherlands does deliver though. There have been karting world champions like Giedo van der Garde and Peter de Bruijn, who also did a lot of driving here, with Jos. Actually the Netherlands is doing a better job than Belgium. We just have Stoffel Vandoorne. He has driven here too by the way. Often, in fact. They all come here. Kimi also raced here. And Lewis.

'Once we started winning with our team, they all came here. With our team, we won prizes all over the world, so you stand out, don't you? Maybe there are better racetracks in France, I don't know. But they all come here. Maybe it's the atmosphere, who knows?'

In general, karting is the gateway to Formula 1, but in Genk it literally is. Lemmens was European champion and the team with which he achieved his success he ran himself. He built up the Genk circuit to its current international status, where major championships for small karts are held. In this way, Genk drew the attention of the most promising youngsters. It started with Jos Verstappen, but after that lots more motorsport young guns arrived. Lemmens has already mentioned Jenson Button and Kimi Räikkönen, but another was Michael Schumacher, who grew up close by in Kerpen, Germany, just 60 miles away.

And then along came Max. Lemmens noticed him immediately. 'If you watch a young footballer dribbling with the ball, you see his skill straight away. Max was like that. Once every 10 or 12 years a boy like that comes along.' And with that he pops another sweet in his mouth.

Outside, karts are lapping. Lemmens glances at the track. That's how it is with motorsport. It's hypnotising. A roaring kart attracts attention. One quick look is enough for him to judge the qualities of its driver. He has seen thousands on his track and simply knows. With Max he saw it very quickly, just as he did with Jos. Both of them are passionate and full of talent.

All of 'his' drivers are equally dear to him, although Max has an edge now because of his long-time friendship with the Verstappens, and because father and son are largely cut from the same cloth. Another for whom he has a soft spot is Alex Zanardi, who lost both his legs in a big crash in 2001, then reinvented himself in handcycling and won four Paralympic gold medals in 2012 and 2016, only to suffer even more severe injuries in 2020 when competing in Italy. Personalities like that touch him.

'Zanardi is a wonderful man. First class. Always polite, friendly and warm. And at 17 he was already an incredible personality.'

So was Max at that age, says Lemmens.

'We asked Max to do the prize-giving at a big race when he was 17, in his first year in Formula 1. He agreed immediately. It was still possible back then. He was interviewed in English. He listened to the journalist and replied, "That's actually three questions you ask." He immediately took over the initiative. "To answer your first question..." And then he replied to two and three. I thought to myself: damn, 17 years old and in perfect English. It makes sense that he was voted Dutch sports personality of the year in 2015. He was completely himself, with great charisma. And a couple of steps ahead of the journalist straight away. With strong reasoning and quick off the mark. Just like he drives.'

Lemmens is reminded of another protégé, Britain's Jenson Button, whom he managed from 1994 to 1997. Button, too, more or less started his career at Genk. 'I knew very quickly that he was going to be a great one in motorsport,' Lemmens says. Jenson became European karting champion in 1997 with a CRG kart run by Team GKS-Lemmens, reached Formula 1 with Williams in 2000 and eventually became World Champion in 2009 driving for Brawn.

Button cherishes warm memories of his time in Genk. The relationship with the track owner was like one between a father and a son. His father, John Button, who died in 2014, became a family friend, just like Jos Verstappen and his son Max.

Jenson also calls these early years 'perhaps the best time of my life'. On his website, he mentions Genk. He describes his last race in karts, the one in which he became European champion at Genk, as the best memory of his karting days.

'But beware,' adds Lemmens. 'He [Button] was serious. Dead serious. All those boys are top athletes prepared to do anything. At a very young age, they realise what they have to do — and not do — to reach the top. They're incredibly ambitious. Most people don't know that. Because, who actually comes to watch a junior-class race, apart from the parents and an occasional coach? These boys know what it takes at a very young age and they can achieve it. They live in a boyhood dream, but only a few actually make it to the top. There are only 20 drivers in Formula 1 but look how many boys are racing karts.

'Jenson was very focused. He did everything needed. He loved our Belgian ice cream, for example, but as he's on the tall side, and every gram counts in karting, he had to restrain himself. He never took more than two scoops of ice cream! Then he would put the spoon aside. To be able to be so self-disciplined at that age is quite something. It shows true character. Those guys all have that. They say that karting gets into your blood and you can't get rid of it. There's nothing you can do about it. And make no mistake, a kart race is really tough.

'Two sprinters, Kevin and Dylan Borlée, European champions in the Belgian 4x400 metres relay team, drive here regularly. Even they notice how hard it is to do a race of 25 laps with full concentration. The effort needed for arms and legs is enormous. And all this happens at a temperature of maybe 35 degrees, because it's always quite warm just above the asphalt while wrapped in thick overalls and wearing a helmet. You have to be physically fit. You will never make it if you don't give it your all and if you're not in top shape.

'Jenson is a triathlete. And then he also trains with the car and in the simulator. Jos was also very strong. An athlete. You have to be an athlete, although this is sometimes underestimated. People think, well, I can easily drive a lap in a car, but that's a misconception.'

Outside, a driver completes his laps in a tight rhythm. Like a waxwork in a remote-controlled car, he shoots through one bend after another. The high-pitched howl of the engine cuts through the silence. He fights himself. Each lap. He knows the times he must beat. It's a lonely battle, one that every driver has with himself, as every sportsman must fight with himself. Yet only in motorsport do external factors play such a large role. And the frustrations that go with them. Is it the engine... is it the track... is it the chassis?

Max and Jos also fought that battle together, here on this Belgian tarmac. The young Max was never alone because he could fall back on his father. Hundredths of a second counted back then too, every lap. The challenge was continuous progress. Faster, better — while moving the body as little as possible. A kart driver who moves around a lot is doing something wrong. He has insufficient control of the machine. A fast lap is like the choreography of a dance, every driver will agree. But a dance at top speed.

'The feeling of speed in a kart is addictive,' says Lemmens. 'You're only a few centimetres above the ground and that makes speeds seem even faster than they actually are. If I tell you that on this track we reach an average speed of 92kph [57mph], with a top speed of around 140kph [nearly 90mph], it's like going 300kph [nearly 190mph]. Just like in a Formula 1 car.'

The competition is ruthless and those who don't have enough talent fall through the cracks.

Big Jenson Button with little Max Verstappen at Genk — a place where
they both learned a lot about race driving.

'It's a very tough sport. I've seen them, the drivers who thought they were good, but none of them could bring that little bit of extra to make it to the top. That top is Formula 1. If you're two tenths of a second short, a blink of an eye, you have no chance. Then you're condemned to the ranks of the amateurs. There's nothing wrong with that, but that's how tough it is. At a European championship, 20 guys circulate within a tenth of a second. And they're all fast, you know. But none of them is Max.

'This brutal competition is also the beauty of this sport. Karting is close racing. Just look' — he gestures to the track — 'how spectacular this place is for someone who likes watching motorsport. You stand outside on the terrace and you can follow everything. That's different from a Formula 1 circuit, where usually you can see only a small section of the track. Here you don't have enough eyes or ears. It's great to see how these guys interact with each other. Real sport. They race side by side and nothing bad ever happens.'

He thinks back to Max and his friends and remembers their sportsmanship.

'When they had gone all the way on the racetrack, they would play football afterwards.'

But still, where did Max make the difference? Lemmens smiles, as if he's being asked to explain how he first discovered the talent of a Messi.

'At the races he was phenomenal. First came Max, and 20 metres behind him the rest followed. I could immediately see that this little man had something special. Of course, I couldn't know that he would make it to Formula 1. But with a father like that, the chance was greater.'

The secret of Genk is perhaps the secret of Max Verstappen. Here on this typical track, of which there seem to be so many in Europe, the Dutch prodigy found his style, just like Button and Räikkönen before him. So what's the secret? Is there a secret?

'There's no secret. Only that I designed the track with a certain vision and from my own experience, plus the experience I had with my team. I wanted a layout that resulted in spectacular racing, where plenty of overtaking was possible. Where the drivers had fun and the public could enjoy a lot of battles.

'I'm sure this is one of the most spectacular tracks in the world. I've never asked, but I feel the drivers like coming here for that reason too. The racing here is special. What's the finest spectacle on a track? When there's overtaking, when there's close racing. Now, close racing happens on most kart tracks, but they usually have fewer braking points. We have six.

'There are better tracks, I'll admit that. But they're wider and have a lot

A particular feature of the Lemmens-designed Genk circuit is the number of overtaking opportunities it offers. The circuit played a significant part in developing this aspect of Max's supreme talent.

of fast corners. The drivers all accelerate and at full speed they aren't that far apart, so there isn't much overtaking. The idea behind this track is that you have to be able to outbrake each other at more sections of the track. And that's exactly what I often see occurring in Max's Formula 1 races.'

He sees more. Paul Lemmens looks at motorsport with the eye of a master. He looks beyond the successful overtaking manoeuvre or the superior cornering technique. That's why he knows that the demands of motor racing are so often seriously underestimated.

'The people who don't know, they think it's so easy.' He looks almost apologetic and points to the lone kart driver out on his track. 'What do you think is going on in his head? That's fighting, every single metre. How do I turn into a corner, where's my braking point, how do I let the kart roll out, at what moment do I hit the gas? But if you start thinking about that, it won't work. It has to be automatic. Max has that. There's no other explanation for it. You can't blame people who only watch races. It's very difficult to grasp it all. The general public see cars moving quickly and one is faster than the other. It's not that simple. Guys like Max have it in their genes. He reads a circuit like no other.'

The field is lining up for the start. The 30–35 karts on the small track together produce a deafening noise. The drivers have their right feet on accelerator pedals, hands on steering wheels. When the starting signal is given, the whole pack rushes towards the first corner. Karts have no mirrors. Drivers only look ahead. Next to, behind and in front of them is a mishmash of karts, with screeching revs and sliding tyres.

'The intuition of these boys is unerring,' observes Lemmens. 'They never look sideways or, even worse, backwards. They hear it when there's a kart next to them. True, there are no mirrors, but looking backwards is a mortal sin. If you do, you're lost, because it's a sign of weakness.'

At the first corner of a Formula 1 Grand Prix, team bosses hold their breath, hoping it will all go well. When the pack gets through that corner, everyone breathes a sigh of relief. In the next one, things are a little easier, because there are slightly bigger gaps between the cars. Max has always been, as Lemmens knows, a master of the start, and of the early laps. He invariably got away first and won.

'Starting strongly and getting through the mêlée without damage is something these guys learn in karting, but Max had that something extra.

He has the qualities of a super-talent, an exceptional racer who knows just what's going on during the first lap. When the tyres are still cold, you need to adapt your style and drive a little differently compared with the rest of the race, without overheating the rubber. Max could do that. His first laps were phenomenal. Usually he had already established a gap and nobody could close that again. That happened not just once, but every time. He found unique lines and knew how to use the tyres faultlessly.'

Karting changed enormously in the period between Jos and Max.

'When Jos was still racing, he adjusted the carburettor while driving. If it had too much fuel, the engine wouldn't run properly on the straight. If the mixture was too lean, the engine would stall.

'A real driver uses 70 percent of his brain capacity to race, the other 30 percent to analyse. A great driver is also 100 percent honest. In motor racing you can easily find reasons why things don't go the way you want. The tyre pressures aren't right, the chassis doesn't steer, the engine doesn't give enough power. You have to be clear about that with the mechanic. If you can't, you're selling yourself short. It's one of the most important things: never compromise, never be too nice. Tell it like it is. You also have to be 100 percent honest with yourself. Even then you cannot compromise. Jos could do that. He knew what the technology was doing and what he was doing. He could say to himself: don't do anything to the set-up because I haven't understood that corner yet.'

In the end, it all comes down to the talent and qualities of the driver.

'Take Senna for example. A kart looks simple, but it requires a lot of fine tuning. The driver has to be able to feel that, to know what's happening at any moment of the race. When you turn, when you come out of the corner, when you're in the middle of the corner. You learn that here and you also need it in Formula 1. The simulator can't teach you that. In the end it's the driver who decides. The more he masters the whole process, the better he gets.

'Senna always said: "50 percent is computer work, 50 percent is me." Kimi's like that too. He's also a phenomenon, one of the outstanding drivers. He has also done a lot of driving here. He can fine-tune a car like no other, get it race-ready. He's renowned for tuning a car. Apart from the computers and the sensors, the best drivers give a lot of input.'

Ayrton Senna was Formula 1 World Champion in 1988, 1990 and 1991. Kimi Räikkönen achieved that in 2007.

CHAPTER 6
THE TYRE PROFESSOR

If there's any sort of stereotype for a small boy with Formula 1 potential, there was little evidence of it on the afternoon when Jos Verstappen paid a visit to his friend Kees van de Grint in the Dutch village of Deil. Little Max was there too but he didn't play with cars and there wasn't a miniature racetrack in the living room, even if van de Grint did have a barn full of classic mopeds and karts. Max just played with toys while the men talked about complicated matters.

Rotterdam-born Kees van de Grint, a well-known tyre specialist in Formula 1, is the intellectual of Dutch motor racing. He seems like a scientist who accidentally ended up in the racing world. Designer glasses, a narrow mouth and friendly eyes add to his distinctive look. He talks gently but decisively. If, during conversation, he's certain about a point he's making, he invariably ends with the word 'so', as if to conclude the matter. He knows what he's talking about.

Ever since his youth, van de Grint has been closely involved with karting. It has become his way of life. Tyres are his job, karts his passion. He has even written a book on the subject, *Alles over 50 Jaar Skelteren & Karten in Nederland* ('Everything about 50 Years of Go-Karting & Karting in the Netherlands'). He's Vice-President of the Commission Internationale de Karting, the karting section of the FIA (Fédération Internationale de l'Automobile), the world's motorsport governing body.

Van de Grint became Michael Schumacher's confidant during the Ferrari years, when a fierce tyre war raged between Bridgestone and Michelin in Formula 1. The Dutchman found himself promoted from karts via single-seaters to the premier class, becoming not just an adviser to the German World Champion but also a friend. He was part of Ferrari's technical staff through the World Championship years from 2000 to 2004 and stayed with the team until 2007.

Ferrari hadn't won a World Championship since 1979 and the *tifosi*, Italy's devoted fans, were losing faith in the Prancing Horse. A dream team was formed around Schumacher, with van de Grint a part of it. In 2000, he was added to the technical staff of the Scuderia, alongside heavyweights such as designer Rory Byrne, technical director Ross Brawn and general manager Jean Todt, who later served as President of the FIA.

Van de Grint had been working for Bridgestone but the Japanese tyre company released him to Ferrari to take up an important role in the complicated tactical and technical tyre game. At the 2004 French Grand Prix at Magny-Cours, he played with fire, joining Schumacher in advocating a bold tyre choice. As a result, the German won the race. 'If he had lost, I could have packed my bags.'

The 'tyre professor' also maintained a warm relationship with his compatriot Jos Verstappen, whom he had known since karting. They shared ambitions. 'When Jos raced for Minardi, we sometimes had secret meetings behind the pits. Of course, we couldn't do that in public, in front of the teams and journalists, but we did meet.' Minardi posed no threat to Ferrari, but team technicians generally remained strictly separated in the paddock.

With Max's arrival in Formula 1, memories of Jos suddenly become relevant again. The outside world saw the youngest Formula 1 driver of all time as 'Project Jos 2.0', as if history was repeating itself, but with the flaws removed. That wasn't quite true, as van de Grint knows. Or maybe not true at all.

'Max simply lived his boyhood dream,' says van de Grint. 'What's better in a child's life than doing just what you want? I think I know Jos well enough to know he was pretty strict and kept up the pressure. That's how I see it. I think Max was just allowed to be a kid and that's how it was. He often played football, but he preferred karting. That makes for a great childhood, doesn't it?'

Moreover, Max has that indomitable spirit that makes it seem as if everything is turned into an advantage. There was no plan, according to the tyre man, no 'Project Max'. It was clear that the young Verstappen was born for Formula 1, but something could easily have gone wrong. It's a long road to that pinnacle of racing, with wrong turns beckoning all the way.

'I remember that after Max's karting career, it was difficult to decide what to do next. In hindsight, it seems as if the whole trajectory was directed from the age of four, but coincidence, circumstances, and money, too, determined the choice.'

The tyre professor's heart is in karting and that's why he has clicked so well with a good few young World Champions. Whether the name was Ayrton Senna, Michael Schumacher or Kimi Räikkönen, meeting van de Grint in the paddock always invited the question: 'How's karting going?'

The combination of tyres and karting is totally unique. Van de Grint can 'read' the rubber like no other. Similarly, a young driver has to develop a feeling for the tyres, a task that the Dutchman judges to be more difficult nowadays. He thinks that excessive regulation is the reason — and this doesn't make for better drivers.

'Max was the last of a generation who was able to benefit from the freedom that existed in karting. Now, all the uniformity in karting is flowing through to Formula 1. This is because the FIA has limited tyre testing in karting, just as it has for the Formula cars. So now there's no more free testing of new material. That was one of the most instructive parts of tyre management. Guys like Kimi Räikkönen or Jarno Trulli still say they learned the most from that period. That certainly applies to Max too.'

Van de Grint knew the young Jos before the Netherlands had ever heard of the Verstappens. On behalf of Bridgestone, he secretly booked the Genk karting circuit in 1988 to try out a new type of tyre with his friend and champion Peter de Bruijn. Nobody else was supposed to be there, but there was a 16-year-old boy hanging around who did some odd jobs for track owner Paul Lemmens.

'That was Jos. He maintained the rental karts and was allowed to use the track for training. Bridgestone, my employer, was the biggest in the karting world, but the competition was on its heels, so something new had to be thought up. We came up with a new tyre, different from the usual one, with a lower profile and naturally a larger rim. It had to be a winner. I created a new design and with Peter we were set to work.

'After the race, a young guy came up to me and introduced himself as Jos Verstappen and asked if I was going back to the Netherlands. I said I was. He

Kees van de Grint — karting guru, tyre specialist and motorsport intellectual.

asked, "May I have a lift?" That was fine by me. I had filled my small van with those new tyres and Jos had to sit between them while we drove. A few weeks later I returned to Genk and saw, to my amazement, that he had had new Tecno rims made, on which the new tyres already fitted. You can guess where that information came from!

"At first I was rather angry, because this was actually secret. But I understood it. Jos was still a junior, yet completely focused on technique and materials. I thought it said something about him. He did everything he could to go faster. He already had that cleverness about the details. Jos also knew that motorsport isn't just a matter of turning the steering wheel but also about trying to get a little bit ahead with the equipment. The great thing was that the following year, at the first race of the season in Montpellier, he won Class A with that tyre.

'A year later, Bridgestone issued a poster that featured him with the text, "We the technology, you the talent." Yet the name Verstappen wasn't familiar in those days. In the early 1990s Jos was just one of many. So in retrospect that poster was almost prophetic.'

Besides Jos's eye for technical details, van de Grint noticed in him the young driver's killer instinct. Everything revolved around winning. It's a character trait that van de Grint now sees in Max.

'Losing wasn't Jos's thing. For him it was all or nothing. The second driver is the first loser. I can still remember a race in Liedolsheim, Germany, where he didn't have to win to become European champion. I said to him: "Jos, take it easy now, third is good enough." He didn't want to hear about that. Full throttle remained his approach. Fortunately, it all worked out, but it could have gone wrong. It didn't matter to him: winning was always the goal. Even if he didn't have to.'

The following year, at the karting world championships in Le Mans, things didn't go well. In front of his future manager Huub Rothengatter, who had travelled to the French race especially for him, Jos collided with Giancarlo Fisichella. He didn't make it to the finish line.

'Jos was already known in karting circles as a great talent, but not yet in bigger leagues. After retiring from his racing career, Huub was looking for a boy he could coach. He came to Le Mans for Jos. Yes, and then things went wrong because Jos wanted to win at all costs. Fortunately, Huub, just like Bridgestone, saw his true talent and took Jos to Frits van Amersfoort. Driving a Formula Opel Lotus car, he proved immediately fast.'

This was a decisive moment in Jos's career, and one that was preceded by plenty of agonising about whether it was the right decision.

It was very similar with Max when he switched from karts to Formula 3. Wasn't that too big a leap and too soon? Wouldn't an intermediate step through Formula Renault have been better? Not in hindsight — but in 2014 that wasn't an easy decision.

'I did talk to Huub about that, because initially there were quite a few doubts,' recalls van de Grint. 'I never felt that way myself. I think Max was ready for it. It's sometimes said that perhaps a learning year is preferable, that if things are moving really fast you should pace yourself more cautiously. I don't believe in that. A learning year is a lost year. If an opportunity presents itself, you shouldn't hesitate for a moment. You should grab it with both hands. Max was able to join Frits in Formula 3 and that was a good choice, as it turned out later. A strong match.'

At an age when some youngsters are dreaming of getting a licence to ride a moped, Max Verstappen stepped into his first single-seater. A 16-year-old in a racing car with 215 horsepower, weighing only around 500kg, with a top speed of 170mph and 0–60mph acceleration in 2.9 seconds. Without traction control and ABS.

Team Verstappen decided upon Formula 3 for the 2014 season after other options had been considered and abandoned. The plan to get Max into Formula 1 accelerated that year. He won ten races for Frits van Amersfoort. The calculated gamble turned out well. The question of whether he could handle Formula 3 physically and mentally was soon answered decisively.

According to Kees van de Grint, the step from a kart to a proper single-seater racing car isn't as big as most people think.

'The fact that both Jos and Max made that switch with great success proves it. And we shouldn't forget stars like Emerson Fittipaldi and Riccardo Patrese, who also instantly excelled. From a kart with a gearbox to a Formula car is a natural transition. The system is the same and if you have this level of talent it will be easy for you.'

Yet it isn't a given that a karting champion will make a successful transition to the next rung of the ladder. There are many examples of young bloods from karting who failed to secure a seat in higher levels of motorsport.

The Netherlands has produced numerous karting champions. To name just a few, Giedo van der Garde, Peter de Bruijn, Peter Koene, Nyck de Vries,

Carlo van Dam and Nicky Pastorelli stand out. But only van der Garde was able to reach Formula 1, and even then just for a single proper season, 2013, with a poor team. Internationally, too, there are numerous examples of superb karting exponents who didn't break through. Becoming world champion in karts is no guarantee of success in Formula 1. Ayrton Senna said that Terry Fullerton, who often beat him in karts, was the best driver he had ever seen, but few have heard of him. It was much the same for Colin Brown when he raced karts against Lewis Hamilton.

These men didn't lack talent, passion, hard work or commitment. They were all phenomenal when racing on smaller wheels.

'What is it then?' I ask. Van de Grint hesitates. Because, even though he's extremely knowledgeable, he doesn't want to pretend that he's the oracle.

'History has proved that the absolute top men of karting have hardly ever achieved anything in Formula 1. So... They've been at the forefront for years, winning by that one tenth of a second. Tuning and racing have gone hand in hand. But for a driver with Formula 1 ambitions, it can be better not to go for karting titles and instead make sure of advancing out of karting in good time. Ayrton Senna wasn't a karting world champion, Alain Prost wasn't a karting world champion, Michael Schumacher wasn't a karting world champion. Other than Max, Riccardo Patrese, Jarno Trulli and Charles Leclerc are the only karting world champions to have won a Grand Prix. Even Lewis Hamilton wasn't a karting world champion, although, I have to be honest, he did have bad luck.

'With Max it has been different. He not only had perfect equipment but also the key ingredient: the talent to win. Guys like Lewis Hamilton, Kimi Räikkönen and Nico Rosberg drove with all of their talent, and if their karts had been prepared by Jos they would have become world champions. Otherwise, I can't explain why every karting champion doesn't become Formula 1 World Champion — except to say there isn't room for everybody on the highest step!'

Van de Grint compares karting with five-a-side indoor football.

'Why are the best indoor footballers from Barcelona not on the pitch in the Camp Nou? It's a different discipline, where technique is much more important than the physical aspect. That's how you should see it with karting.'

Does that make it more difficult to recognise true talent?

'Yes, you can only do that if you have first-hand experience, if you have coached a boy for years, and know the circumstances under which he has achieved those victories. The statistics alone don't tell you much. That's scoreboard journalism. It's all about the facts behind it. You also have to look at consistency and the equipment. I get a bit tired of all those people who claim they saw Max's talent at an early age. Of course they did. Even a blind person could see that. The teams were lining up for him. No, it's much harder to spot a boy who doesn't finish first all the time.'

Helmut Marko is regarded as a smart talent scout in Formula 1 as adviser to Red Bull and the man behind the formation of the Toro Rosso 'junior' team. Marko brought Sebastian Vettel, Daniel Ricciardo, Daniil Kvyat, Carlos Sainz Jr and Max Verstappen into Formula 1.

'Talent hunters?' continues van de Grint. 'Well, may I put that in perspective? I once tipped a driver to Jean Todt when he was the boss of Ferrari. I told him to go for it. If Ferrari had to sign him later on, they would have to pay a lot of money. His name? Nico Rosberg. I also realised that Lewis pushed the throttle a little harder, to put it simply, but for me Nico was just a bit better. Then I also said to Todt, "You have to keep an eye on him." Well, they didn't — and the rest is history.'

At the end of 2015 and the beginning of 2016, Rosberg started winning race after race. In the van de Grint household, this was quietly celebrated.

'Yes, I did enjoy that, to be honest. It shows how relative everything is. Also it's often guesswork. Not everything is within your control. Just as in football. How many wrong purchases have top teams made? Talent is no guarantee and certainly not in the world of Formula 1, where there's much more to it than just driving ability. If, like me, you have been very close to a couple of drivers, well, you get some perspective on that. If a footballer takes a good free kick, it doesn't mean that a coach can also work well with him. Those guys in Formula 1 also have to be good at communicating. When I worked with Nico, I noticed that he was not only fast but also very clever. I don't think Michael [Schumacher] was the fastest driver ever. Senna was perhaps the fastest. But Michael was the best. He could win races that were impossible to win. He could lead a team and motivate people to go to the limit.

'I've been lucky in my career to work with a lot of huge talents and top performers. Whether it was Hamilton, Rosberg, Schumacher or Räikkönen, those guys all did karting. As a Bridgestone engineer, I was always looking for the best drivers — because they were able to provide good test results. They weren't necessarily the champions. Kimi wasn't leading the pack when we picked him up, nor was Nico Hülkenberg. Nico was sixth or seventh in

Working for Japanese tyre company Bridgestone, Kees van de Grint was a key
component in Michael Schumacher's all-conquering period at Ferrari.

a race when he caught my eye, because that sixth place was a really good result considering his machinery. In my view, that was relatively a better performance than the winner's and I knew immediately that I had to watch this guy. That way I could invite the right drivers for the tyre tests.'

Kees van de Grint has known three generations of Verstappens, back to Max's grandfather Frans, who died in November 2019, and including his mother Sophie. He has plenty to say about all of them.

'Sophie did some testing for Bridgestone. She drove in Formula Super A and won the Margutti Trophy in Parma. That's not a walk in the park, you know. She didn't continue her career in karting, but she was ridiculously good. She won races among the stars. There have been three women in karting who have been equal to the men: Lotte Helberg, Sophie Kumpen and Susy Raganelli.

'And Grandpa Frans. I had such a laugh with him. A very nice man, but he couldn't count to ten before uttering something. That's not always appreciated in the world of Formula 1. Team bosses have huge egos. If you don't follow their lead, you can leave. In Formula 1, politics always play a role in the background. Jos also learned from his mistakes and Max took advantage of that. Plus he has a lot of his mother's side in him.

'The Verstappens are ordinary people in an unattainable branch of sport. That's what makes them so unique. They're pure. Authentic. And that's why they're so popular. Yes, sometimes emotions play a role, but that's okay. It soon passes. I've had a bit of an argument with Jos because he disagreed with a choice of tyres. But the tension had gone after an hour.

'They have a fan club that's bigger than that of a professional football club. It's really no exaggeration to say that the Verstappens have had an enormous impact on Dutch people. The way Max now deals with his fame is fantastic. Max always looks neat. It's a fresh look.

'The difference between Jos and Max? Max has a lot of Sophie and that makes him an amiable person, I think. The difference between them is that Jos could have won races and Max became World Champion.'

Between 2000 and 2003, Kees van de Grint worked at Ferrari while Jos Verstappen drove for Arrows and Minardi. The gulf between them couldn't have been wider. Ferrari was unbeatable while Jos fought at the back of the pack. They flew all over the world, repeatedly meeting each other, in Melbourne, Kuala Lumpur or São Paulo. Jos had to latch onto fleeting hopes while Kees was experiencing big-time winning.

'Our roles weren't comparable of course. Relatively speaking, I had it a lot easier. But I did gain enormous admiration for Jos in those days and I still have that. Just think: he was a great performer in karts and won nine times out of ten, then he got into Opel Lotus and won, then into Formula 3 and won. And then he arrived in Formula 1 knowing he had the talent to win, but it didn't work out. His equipment held him back. To go through that for ten years... well, hats off to him.

'In his final few years he still sometimes managed to rise above it all and excel. With Arrows, there were the times when he got into the points. With Minardi, he set the fastest time on a wet Friday at Magny-Cours. Those were the moments that kept him coming back. Those were top-class performances.

'It was also a political matter why Jos didn't end up with a big team. How was it possible that a man like David Coulthard stayed so long at McLaren? In football a guy like him would have been replaced much earlier. What about Jarno Trulli, Ralf Schumacher or Heinz-Harald Frentzen? I don't think Jos was inferior to any of them. It's intriguing how the mechanisms work in a multi-million industry — how the choices are made. I've said before that Formula 1 claims to be high-tech but there are conservative minds in charge.'

Van de Grint mentions the profligacy of Formula 1, where millions are thrown away seemingly carelessly as a result of wrong choices.

'Because so much money is involved, politics plays a big role. Rather than hiring a grafter who can drive brilliantly, sometimes racing teams would rather have a personable guy who does well with the sponsors, brings in some money himself, and is politically correct and malleable. That, too, is motor racing.'

In the case of Max Verstappen, everything has come together. Talent, charm, manners, speed. That too can make a difference in the complicated interplay of powers. As the Dutch rock 'n' roll star Herman Brood sang, 'If you win you have friends'.

'That's a truism,' concludes van de Grint. 'At Ferrari I know that the cars of Rubens [Barrichello] and Michael [Schumacher] were 99.9 percent the same and they both had the same choice of tyres, but because Michael always won the team worked just that little bit harder for him. That's what I mean.'

CHAPTER 7
SECRET VISIT TO WALES

In search of Max Verstappen's roots, a visit to Westmaas, in the hinterland of Rotterdam, isn't really an obvious choice. This sleepy village of 2,000 inhabitants in the rural Hoeksche Waard lies just a few miles south of one of the world's largest ports, yet life here seems to be at a standstill. There are farms, small dykes and nature in abundance, especially around the Zwanegat and the Binnenbedijkte Maas. It doesn't get any more Dutch than this.

Tucked away on a small industrial estate is MP Motorsport. This is where Jos Verstappen and Sander Dorsman, who runs MP Motorsport, had their first exploratory discussion in 2013. The subject was Max's first test in a racing car.

MP Motorsport isn't very well known to people around here. In fact, in neighbouring Klaaswaal a resident working in his garden was unable to provide directions. He just shrugged his shoulders — never heard of it. Yet MP Motorsport is one of the top two racing teams in the Netherlands, an operation with international recognition, a multi-million-pound business. All that is invisible from the outside.

Week in week out, all year round, racing cars are prepared for action, for testing and racing. They come and go regularly as they travel to and from races. This seems to go unnoticed in the surrounding area, perhaps even throughout entire region.

Dutch boys — and they are almost exclusively boys — dream of being able to drive for Dorsman. Perhaps, eventually, they will move up to the top echelon of motor racing, the one in which their role model Max Verstappen races.

Dorsman's mission is to train and deliver as much young talent as possible for the next generation of motor racing. This is where the new Lewis Hamiltons and Sebastian Vettels might come from, the youngsters who will step into the shoes of the old hands nearing the end of their careers.

Dorsman believes that Formula 1 could do with a few new faces. He would like to see the regulations opened out. More cars in the races, perhaps as many as 30 of them. More youngsters in the field, amidst the experienced. With the 'Max Factor' reverberating through the Netherlands, Dorsman has a good few protégés ready go — and more coming up behind.

'We try to help talented young drivers find a future in motorsport,' says the quietly spoken Dorsman. 'Of course, Formula 1 is the best, the highest aspiration, but many boys end up in other classes, where they can earn a good living. In those cases, our mission is accomplished as well.'

From this motorsport breeding ground, indeed, other promising youngsters have emerged hot on the heels of Max Verstappen. Let's briefly go back to 2016. Aged just 15, Richard Verschoor was included in Red Bull's junior team that year. After his victory in the Formula 4 race supporting the Russian Grand Prix at Sochi, Red Bull's Helmut Marko personally summoned him to the hospitality unit in the paddock. Just a few hours earlier, Verschoor, together with equally talented team-mate Jarno Opmeer and third driver Danny Kroes, had been given a tour of the Toro Rosso pits by Max Verstappen. One week later, Max was promoted to Red Bull.

Sochi 2016 suddenly meant a lot to Dutch motorsport. Dorsman enjoyed the occasion. Three young drivers from his team had an audience with the great Max, who was only 18 himself.

'It was as if they were visiting Michael Jackson,' remembers Dorsman. 'They looked up to Max, even though there was only a three-year difference in age. Max probably remembered clearly how he acted at their age. The boys would have been satisfied with a handshake, a photo and 15 minutes of his time. But they were allowed to stay for two hours. Max took all the time he needed. That was really nice to see.'

P Motorsport has become a household name in Dutch racing. The team has been around since 1995, when it started out in Formula Ford — the prime 'feeder' series back then. In 2013, it moved up

Sander Dorsman — the man who gave Max his first test
in a single-seater racing car.

to GP2, which at that time was the category immediately below Formula 1. Nowadays MP Motorsport is a major player in international racing and still competes one level below Formula 1, in the FIA Formula 2 Championship, as well as in Formula Renault 2.0 and Formula 4. Whether the ultimate step — going into Formula 1 — could ever happen remains to be seen, because the investment required would be many times greater than the team's current budget.

There's one other thing about MP Motorsport that's very special. It was the first team to let Max Verstappen drive a racing car — a Formula Renault 2.0 car. It became an unforgettable day.

Motorsport journalist Allard Kalff brought the parties together. It began with his plan to have Jos Verstappen do a demonstration run in a GP2 car during the Masters meeting at Zandvoort in 2013, 20 years after Jos's victory in the Marlboro Masters of Formula 3 event at the circuit. For various reasons, it didn't happen. When Kalff called Jos to cancel the arrangement, Jos told him he wanted Max to have a test in a Formula Renault. Kalff contacted Dorsman.

'I told him that Jos wanted Max to try a Formula Renault car, but privately,' says Kalff. 'Could he arrange that? And I gave him Jos's number. That's all I did. The two came into contact and Sander let Max have one of those expensive tests, which normally cost a few thousand Euros.'

Dorsman confirms Kalff's account.

'The world of Dutch motorsport is very small. Everyone knows each other. Allard [Kalff] and I keep in touch. Sometimes we have coffee or lunch together, and there's always plenty to discuss. Allard told me that Max was still involved in karting and wanted to come and have a look around with us. I phoned Jos and offered him a free test.

'Jos dropped by and we went through the whole thing. It's quite a big logistical operation to get a car to a circuit. One condition was that it had to remain a secret. If we were to do it at Zandvoort, the whole world would know about it and people would draw conclusions. That wouldn't be fair on Max either. You have to let a boy like that do his first laps in peace, without enormous media pressure.'

Tony Shaw is a respected engineer in motorsport. With his wife Sarah, he ran the successful Manor Competition team in the British Formula Renault Championship, with numerous successes that famously included maiden single-seater crowns for Kimi Räikkönen (2000) and Lewis Hamilton (2003).

When Formula Renault dried up on the British scene at the end of 2011, Shaw looked for a new opportunity and joined MP Motorsport.

Shaw suggested a fairly remote circuit in South Wales that would be suitable for Max's test. There would be no journalists around and, if someone did get wind of what was going on, the circuit could be closed off. It was also small, just a mile and a half in length, and quite tightly configured so that the crew could see a good amount of the track and closely observe a young driver in action.

Pembrey is used extensively for testing as well as racing, and for numerous categories — single-seaters, touring cars, sports cars, motorcycles, karts and even trucks. Although some people regard it as a 'Mickey Mouse' track, it's quite technical and demanding. It is, in Dorsman's words, 'the perfect location to explore'.

Dorsman and Shaw hired Pembrey for two days in October 2013. Two days that were to be used entirely for Max to get acquainted with a racing car, in order to determine which direction he should take: Formula Renault, Formula 3 or GP2.

A feature of Formula Renault is that testing can take place anywhere and at any time. Whereas testing for other classes is tightly regulated by the FIA, Formula Renault teams can go their own way, as long as budget allows it. Normally a test like Max Verstappen's at Pembrey would have to be paid for, but Dorsman wanted to make an exception in this special case.

'It coincided with our annual schedule, so we could do it. One day before the test we fitted the seat, as is usual in single-seaters. The next day we were going to drive, but it was raining. That was very annoying because you can't get the best out of the car's systems.'

He couldn't have guessed that the Dutch 16-year-old's mysterious first laps would be so significant. Although no journalists were present, Frits van Eldik, a veteran motorsport photographer, was invited to attend and took a few jealously guarded and historically important photos for Team Verstappen's own use.

Max's car carried number 23 and was finished in orange, white and black with little splashes of bright green on the mirrors. When he lowered himself into the car, his expression seemed tense, his eyes bright and concentrated.

Max recorded his memories a year or two later in an anniversary book published to celebrate 20 years of MP Motorsport: 'I didn't know what to expect. There were sheep and birds everywhere. I think I hit a lot of birds as well. The car sounded very loud to me.'

Dorsman: 'The uniqueness of that moment is difficult to describe. You don't realise it, yet you're experiencing something very special. Of course, you see that the boy is super-fast and picks up Tony Shaw's advice easily. But you don't know yet what will happen later. Max is one young man amongst many, you initially think. We have a lot of them running around.

'I have to admit that I couldn't quite work out why I suspected that here was a special driver at work. He was fast. People around the track said he had broken the lap record. Well, I thought at the time, it sounds good but of course it doesn't tell you that much, because you don't know the conditions in which previous records were set.

'Tony Shaw, however, was hysterical. He had previously tested with Lewis Hamilton and Kimi Räikkönen, but he felt that Max picked up everything even better. He understood quickly, he was fast, and could cope well with changing circumstances.'

On the first day it rained heavily. On the second day the track dried quickly and Max got his first chance to lap on slick tyres.

Kalff: 'I experienced *déjà vu*. Jos reacted to that test in the same way that Huub had reacted to Jos's driving. The enthusiasm, and the fact that things were going so quickly, was overwhelming. I found that strange, to be honest.'

Back in Westmaas, things returned to normal. But the realisation that something special had happened would stay with Dorsman for a long time.

'It's great to be able to say that Max picked it up even better than Hamilton,' concludes Dorsman. 'But that also creates certain expectations. In my opinion, there are no guarantees in Formula 1. Too many other factors play a role: money, team, circumstances. But how Max drove in Wales was exemplary — and fantastic for his racing career.

'Even when you have masses of data at your disposal, there can still be a gut feeling that tells you something special is happening. That was the case with Max.'

CHAPTER 8
DESTINATION FLORIDA

Will Buxton, the British Formula 1 TV presenter and reporter who features prominently in the hit Netflix documentary *Drive to Survive*, was 33 years old when he first tried single-seater racing. During that experience he became acquainted with a young Dutch driver less than half his age, someone who remained unknown to the world at large but within motorsport now had a reputation that preceded him. This, of course, was Max Verstappen. Buxton was given an unparalleled lesson in motor racing. In all respects.

'If you want to do your job well as a motorsport journalist,' says Buxton, 'you don't just watch Formula 1. You watch everything: Formula 2, Formula 3, Formula 4... developments in karting, everything... Motorsport is a relatively small world, where rumours circulate quickly. And as a journalist, you want to be the first to discover the new kid on the block. In our little world, stories went round that there were great talents on the way — Charles Leclerc and Max Verstappen. Stories that when you heard them second-hand almost took on a mythical form and became larger than life. Then you want to see with your own eyes what's going on, if all those stories are true. That was the reason I went to Palm Beach for one of the rounds of the 2014 Florida Winter Series. Although, I have to say, the organisation also invited me to drive one of those cars — and you never turn down an offer like that.'

For Buxton, the driving itself was thrilling — who wouldn't echo that if given the chance? — but just as fascinating was the insight he gained into racecraft. At the end of each session, the participants saw the data about their performances in detail. Should they ever have had the illusion that they had driven fast, they were quickly brought back to earth by the harsh reality.

As such, the data of the 33-year-old rookie was compared with that of the teenagers. The differences? Astronomical.

'After each session you could go through the data with the engineers. In a kind of classroom, you would go through the videos of your performance with a coach. Then these so-called "data overlays" were used, enabling you to compare where the other drivers' braking points were, and when another driver would hit the gas pedal.'

This was a fascinating glimpse into the inner world of motorsport, one that was extremely useful to a motorsport reporter because of the benefits from all that new knowledge. As for the data, some of it was shocking. Not for Buxton, who had no illusions about his abilities, but for the other competitors. They included Lance Stroll and Nicolas Latifi.

'I think that's when Max started to get under everybody's skin,' says Buxton. 'They could see from all this public data, which revealed all the nuances of driving style, that this kid was doing things with the car that they couldn't. Braking later, on the throttle earlier — that's what he was doing. He managed to get more speed out of a corner and onto a straight. It was really special.

'Antonio Fuoco, who already had experience with Max in Formula 3, hated him. He really did. They were constantly having incidents with each other, cutting each other off, and Max was always beating him. Max still drove like a kart racer. He tailed people's rear wings closely, nudging in the corners. Not everyone liked that, because that style of driving isn't usual in Formula 3, where you give each other more space. Max emitted this rawness. He was so fast and talented that it frustrated the others. And they knew that. They saw that here was a kid who was light years ahead.'

Apart from the track time, Buxton also had plenty of opportunity to hang out with the Dutch youngster.

'He already had an enormous aura about him. There had been so much talk about Max. The son of a great racer, who won everywhere he went, a racer who would change the world. That had been exactly the case with Lewis Hamilton. Those who had followed Max since his early days in karting shouted to anyone who would listen: this guy is going to be World Champion! It's an easy call to make, as often happens when an apparent talent more or

Palm Beach, February 2014: Will Buxton and Max Verstappen have a laugh
before they take part in the weekend's three races. Max won the last
of the three — his very first single-seater victory.

less breaks through — but those are just words. Jos was his natural reference and, to be honest, wasn't World Champion material. So this was different from Damon Hill [son of double World Champion Graham) or Jacques Villeneuve [son of fabled Ferrari driver Gilles].

'Jos was a brilliant racer and his mother Sophie was also a capable one — but genes don't win races. Do you know how it usually works? If everybody talks about it, that there's a Max Verstappen on the way, then people start to listen.

'My first impression was that he seemed a really nice guy. Friendly, easy to talk to. But how do you expect a 16-year-old to be? Some guys who come straight from karting have so much self-confidence that it looks like arrogance. That wasn't the case at all with Max. He was always relaxed and easy-going. And we had a lot of time to talk to each other.'

Buxton was able to benefit from that. The first journalist to embrace a new talent will always be a friend, no matter how great the talent later becomes, no matter how much fame he acquires. That first recognition from an outsider does persist. A nod of recognition, an easy rapport — even if personal contact is scarce amidst the media frenzy of Formula 1.

'Yes, in the first year I did benefit from it to some extent, but of course that diminishes later on. It isn't like the old days, when you could approach a driver and have a chat. But at Spa, when he'd just signed for Red Bull and many people didn't yet know him, because there were hardly any photos of him, he was still really enthusiastic. That was fun. Only six months earlier we'd been together in Florida; now he was walking around here like a real Red Bull Formula 1 driver.

'I wanted an interview with him and he took his time, while a mountain of curious people gathered around us. Earlier in the year he had been at Silverstone with his father but nobody paid any attention to him. He was just a pimply faced kid in a school shirt that was way too big. And here he was at Spa, in his Red Bull outfit, with the cap, totally in the mould of a Formula 1 driver. I thought that was great.'

Will Buxton wasn't the only journalist to join the show in Florida. *Top Gear*'s Ollie Marriage also witnessed the birth of a world star in the 'Sunshine State'. The headline of his article published on the *Top Gear* website on 20 August 2014 reads 'Why F1 should fear Max Verstappen'. So it was that these two Brits got one over their Dutch media equivalents, who were still slumbering in blissful ignorance. Buxton and Marriage also experienced something that Dutch journalists could only dream about: they were allowed to drive on the same track as Max Verstappen. Each of the two British journalists was invited to race at one of the rounds and they were able to watch the battle unfold in front of their cockpits, like moviegoers in a 3D cinema. On the *Top Gear* blog, Marriage wrote with a sense of irony and understatement: 'I raced Max Verstappen.'

The Tatuus FA010B Formula Abarth cars used for the Florida Winter Series weren't child's playthings. The Italian-made Tatuus was a fully-fledged racing car with a 1.4-litre turbo engine delivering 190bhp, a six-speed gearbox, and adjustable front and rear wings. It was an FIA-approved racing car for the junior class.

The field in which the British journalists were allowed to show their skills otherwise comprised young hotshoes. Marriage wrote: 'Max won the race, which was pretty much a foregone conclusion. And not against a bunch of track-day wimps, but the cream of the crop of the world's young drivers.'

Many of these drivers were the top talents of the Ferrari Driver Academy, an initiative that had been started by the famed Scuderia Ferrari a few years earlier to promote young drivers within its organisation. The Florida Winter Series was, in effect, a private racing championship with an invited guest or two, the most notable of whom was Max Verstappen. The series comprised four rounds — one each at Sebring and Palm Beach followed by two at Homestead — in a four-week period in January and February, with three races at each round.

Eleven drivers took part in the entire series. Three of them were newly crowned champions from 2013: 19-year-old Raffaele 'Lello' Marciello was FIA European Formula 3 Champion, 18-year-old Ed Jones was European F3 Open Champion and 17-year-old Antonio Fuoco had just won the Formula Renault 2.0 ALPS Series. Lance Stroll, aged only 15 and destined for Formula 1, was making his single-seater racing début after karting success. The others included strong competitors in the shape of Nicolas Latifi and Dennis van de Laar, the latter a relative senior at the age of 20.

A total of 11 young guns, with more than enough eagerness and ambition, bursting with talent and killer instinct. But there was one who stood out above the rest.

The Dutch driver in car number 3 was distinguished not only by his driving skills but also his personality. Unlike everyone else apart from Stroll, Max

Verstappen had no experience of single-seaters in a racing environment, but he quickly proved his qualities: mature, confident, purposeful, focused.

Van de Laar was Max's first team-mate in Florida. The rules dictated that two drivers were put together as pairs and they worked together with one engineer. The logical consequence of this was that data could be shared, which was the most normal thing in the world at Prema Power, van de Laar's team. Braking points, corners, apexes, differences in speed at different points of the track — everything. Van de Laar eagerly absorbed the science behind it like a sponge. After practice sessions and races, all data was superimposed and the two drivers could see how they differed.

'Max immediately went flat out,' recalls Buxton. 'Straight away he had the right feeling with that car, as he had had with karts. In karting there's also work with data but much less of it. So Max was still pretty open-minded. He just got in the car and drove it.

'At first he drove the car like a kart, where you're almost glued together with your opponent, and a brush here and there isn't so bad. You can't do that with a Formula car, because then the front wing comes off. That's what happened on the first weekend. He drove quite aggressively, in that he immediately showed his talent. Within one weekend he had mastered it. He made huge steps.

'Mind you, the first time he sat in the car and drove out of the pitlane was funny. He got a message on his steering wheel and looked at it — and went into the back of Fuoco's car stopped at the red light.'

The first race of the series, at Sebring, was won by van de Laar. It's a victory that he still cherishes as a unique highlight in his career, one that he can look back upon with pride. After all, he's the only Dutchman ever to have beaten Max Verstappen. Max was in front but then it started to rain.

'One of my stronger points,' says Dennis, 'is making the transition between slicks and intermediate tyres. The three of us were fighting for the last corner. Max made a mistake and I was able to pass him and win that race. That was really great. During that championship, where everything was about education, competition and racing, I took big steps forward. Everyone did, I think. It was a great learning experience.'

Of all the drivers, Max attracted the most attention. Ollie Marriage was stunned. Music critic and record producer Jon Landau once wrote: 'I've seen the future of rock 'n' roll and his name is Bruce Springsteen.' Marriage's quote — 'Why F1 should fear Max Verstappen' — is a little less powerful but the

The 12 racers at Palm Beach. Back row from left: Will Buxton, Lance Stroll,
Max Verstappen, Dennis van de Laar, Vasily Romanov and Alex Bosak.
Front row from left: Tatiana Calderón, Nicolas Latifi, Ed Jones,
Raffaele Marciello, Antonio Fuoco and Takashi Kasai.

message is the same. It could just as easily have read: 'I've seen the future of Formula 1 and his name is Max Verstappen.' Perhaps Marriage wasn't aware of Landau's quote and, had he been, maybe he would have adopted it. After all, the English, like no other people in the world, can turn a sense of understatement into pure admiration.

Marriage's outing in the Florida Winter Series came in the final round at Homestead, just south of Miami. The British journalist circulated at the back of the 12-car field and struggled to get his timing right, but a crash course helped him to master the basics. He had a good view ahead to the infamous Turn One, where the infield part of the circuit turns off the speedway. It's a bumpy left-hand kink taken at full speed, 140mph, followed by quite a sharp 80mph left-hander.

'It was all I could do to hang on to the pack and get the line right,' Marriage wrote on his *Top Gear* blog. 'Ahead I saw Max draft up behind another car and send it up the inside of not just him, but another three cars in the space of as many metres.

'I couldn't conceive of how time, distance and physics would permit such a move, let alone the bravery, confidence and skill level needed to not only consider it, but attempt it and make it stick to perfection. I was gobsmacked. Properly impressed.'

The journalist had already had a taste of Verstappen's bravado.

'Max, I quickly gathered, was the bane of the instructors' lives. He questioned everything, wasn't afraid to argue his point and rarely backed down. For a 16-year-old he was remarkably self-assured.

'He got away with it chiefly because, even among a group of 11 seriously talented young racers out to prove themselves, he was a genius on the track.'

Afterwards, Marriage went to talk to Max's father, who in England is nicknamed, like Springsteen, 'The Boss' — Jos The Boss. Together with manager Huub Rothengatter, Jos tried to entice the journalist into a wager: 'Bet he'll be in Formula 1 before 2017?' Marriage jokingly replied: 'No, I won't, because I think he'll be there before that.'

Dennis van de Laar can relate to Ollie Marriage's anecdote. He, too, was impressed by his Dutch compatriot: 'He came to Florida as a young kart racer and left as a thoroughbred Formula 3 driver.'

Van de Laar also made it into Formula 3, with the Prema Power racing team, which at that time was owned by billionaire Lawrence Stroll, father of

Lance. But then Dennis's motor racing career came to an abrupt end. Why? Because of Max?

'I wouldn't go that far, but when you come into contact with boys of that calibre, you have to think twice. The ultimate goal, reaching Formula 1, is only reserved for a very small group. Guys who really have everything. Guys like Max. I'm quite realistic. I don't kid myself too easily. The big goal, Formula 1, wasn't for me. When I was in Formula 3, I could get pretty close to the quick times after a long day of testing, but I needed plenty of time to get everything right.

'Max could be at his top level within three, four, five laps on a new circuit, one he had never even seen before. All of his braking points would be right, acceleration perfectly timed, all of the cornering, taking the apex. He could get the maximum out of the car. I was braking two metres earlier and my cornering speed was 5kph slower. I ended up spending a long time on the track, trying to find the perfect lines and rhythm, while he was already there, giving him time to continue improving the car. He was also very good at communicating what needed to be done. He went the extra mile in that respect as well.

'If a team had called me back then, with an offer to join a junior programme, I wouldn't have hesitated for a moment. I would have said "yes" straight away, put down the phone, burst into cheers and danced for joy.'

At Team Verstappen they did things differently. No dancing for joy — just careful step-by-step progress to Formula 1.

'I'm sure they already had offers,' continues van de Laar, 'but they waited for the right moment. All the Formula 1 teams were vying for him. One of the best decisions Jos and the team made was to postpone that decision as long as possible. When he was in karts, he could already have gone anywhere. Everything would have been paid for him. But they kept it all in their own hands. Then the moment came, and they could choose the team that would really bring Max to Formula 1.'

Mercedes had already made Max an offer he couldn't refuse. But he did. From the outset, the Verstappens were aiming for a proper seat in Formula 1, not a junior programme with all the risks that entailed. His development at Mercedes would have been cautious, perhaps even ending up in DTM, and then there was the possibility of him disappearing from view. That route didn't suit Team Verstappen's plans. It was clear from the start: only the guarantee of driving in a Formula 1 team was acceptable.

Despite what he said earlier, for a while van de Laar did believe in his own Formula 1 ambitions. After all, he had a Formula 3 contract in his pocket, he was going to drive for a top team, he trained hard. All the lights were on green. But if you start racing at the age of 15, as he did, you're too late, even if it wasn't obvious at the time. He was a fast learner. In Formula Renault he drove against guys like Stoffel Vandoorne, Carlos Sainz Jr and Daniil Kvyat, and kept up with them.

'First you notice that you're 10 years behind those guys. They were all in karts from the age of five. But thanks to some very good coaching I was able to make progress very quickly. Then you start to believe in it.'

If you don't come from karts, he now knows, you just have to work even harder. After finishing at school, he went to Italy to further his career there. Racing was his passion and he was on course to make it his profession.

'I had a really special year in Italy with Prema. Physical training every day, cycling, running, mental training, working with the team, learning the technical aspects of the car with the guys at the factory, spending a year in another country — all very instructive. Except, after three years in Formula 3, I realised there was no point in investing any more in trying to reach Formula 1.

'So when the opportunity came along to do something as an entrepreneur, I grabbed it. Racing didn't fit into my life anymore and I called it a day. It was a difficult decision and I hope to return to racing one day. I think I would quickly get used to it again. Endurance racing at Le Mans would be fantastic.'

Van de Laar knows that sums of money with many zeros went down the drain. The quest to be a professional racing driver is expensive and can only be done with significant financial backing. He had Randstad, Williams's major sponsor, behind him, amongst others. That wasn't enough.

'In the end it comes down to pure talent. No more and no less. And you can't buy that. You have to do it all yourself. That also applied to Max. He had to do it himself.

Let's return to January 2014, when Dennis van de Laar still believed in a Formula 1 future. Participating in the Florida Winter Series was one of the best experiences of his life. Not only because of the motor racing, which brought his first race victory, but also the social life, fine weather and even some sightseeing.

He played football with Max and tennis with Jos. He spent time gliding through the Everglades in a motorboat with Max also on board, visiting a crocodile farm. It seems like it was a holiday.

'It may seem so and it really was a fantastic time,' says Dennis, smiling. 'But that doesn't take away from the fact that we were there mainly to race, to gain all the knowledge we needed for the future. Jos and Huub [Rothengatter] and Raymond [Vermeulen] and Max were always there. It was training, racing, getting involved with the team, qualifying, focusing. But I would be lying if I said that it wasn't fun. We lived a good life. Nice hotels, everything well taken care of, food and drinks too. But on the track we went hard.'

The mental challenge and resilience that motor racing entails at any level is almost incomprehensible to an outsider.

'Motor racing is actually a 24/7 commitment with more disappointments than joys,' continues van de Laar. 'Only one driver can win and the rest lose. You really have to be able to cope with that. The motivation has to come entirely from within yourself. Every corner, every lap, every qualifying session — it's all a battle with yourself. You have to go faster and faster. Some people are better able to cope with that than others.

'I didn't handle the pressure as well as Max did. I tend to perform slightly worse when there's pressure. Max seems to feed off it. That seemed very strange. For me, relaxed situations worked better. When I did my laps and there was no pressure, I could drive at my best. In qualifying, which is particularly important in Formula 3 because it determines your starting position for three races, there was pressure. I wasn't able to cope with that so well. I was mentally vulnerable. With Max it went better. I noticed that when we were together in America, and I also see it now, in Formula 1.

'I would find it very difficult if I knew that 500 people in a team were looking over my shoulder and every moment could be seen on television. If the driver makes a mistake, the whole team is beaten — and in front of the world. I don't think Max feels any pressure at all. He puts on his helmet and forgets all about it. The only thing that counts then is racing. It's a quality that only the greats have.'

The mental aspect of motor racing is so often underestimated, as van de Laar has learned and recognised. Racing at the highest level is not only physically demanding but also a psychological obstacle course, littered with doubts, as well as clues about how to improve and learn. It's all about processing a relentless stream of information.

'Everything is analysed and you're constantly confronted with facts. There's

Working for NBC, the American television network, Will Buxton interviews
Max at the 2016 Hungarian Grand Prix.

no hiding from it. You have to process and remember all the data and its disappointments. From ideal lines to the best braking points. Just operating the steering wheel, which has so many buttons. It's so easy to say, "Sure, you just sit in a car, accelerate and steer", but it's more complicated than that.'

Max Verstappen caused another stir when he was heading for Formula 1. At the age of just 16, was he sufficiently strong and fit physically to race at the highest level?

'In hindsight, you can judge that he was,' says van de Laar. 'Beforehand it was less clear. I can imagine that experienced drivers had their doubts. He hadn't fully matured. I've never driven in Formula 1, so it's difficult to judge, but I've been in the professional simulator at Williams. That's a state-of-the-art simulator, with all the technical and digital capabilities of a Formula 1 car. It even has G-forces and replicates track imperfections. All the data from the car during a race weekend is streamed directly into the thing and the strategy is devised with it. The only element missing is gusts of wind, but everything else is the same. Physically it was comparable to the forces that the body has to process in a Formula 1 race, for an hour and a half.

'I experienced it in Formula 3 at Brands Hatch, in a half-hour race. In the first turn at that circuit, the G-force is highest when you go downhill at full throttle: 4.5G — your head becomes 4.5 times heavier. Once, in Barcelona, I found that I couldn't keep my head upright. It was leaning against the edge of the monocoque and I couldn't raise it. Briefly I couldn't see where I was going. You have to be physically very strong, because only then are you mentally strong as well. The moment you have problems somewhere in your body, in your forearms, or in your neck, it has an effect on your mental state. Then you can't be as quick.

'So I can well imagine there were drivers who thought Max was too young. They rightly expressed their concerns, because his motor skills wouldn't have been quite up to scratch. Hamilton said about himself that he was only ready when he reached 22.

'Max has stretched the limits. He didn't suffer from that kind of thing at all, he just did it. Look, normally someone of 16 isn't ready for Formula 1. It definitely isn't the case that any 16-year-old could do it just because he has been karting since he was four years old. Not just any karts, but competition karts. Have you ever driven a kart with a few friends just for fun? After half an hour everyone is worn out, bruised and sore. Karting is physically very demanding and that laid the foundation for what he could do later.'

'Our journey through the Sunshine State took us to evocative tracks: Sebring International Raceway, Palm Beach International Raceway and Homestead Miami, all tough challenges. We were part of a sort of circus that went from track to track, race to race. It was a wonderful time — and above all very instructive. In between there was time for relaxation, but at the same time the schedule was packed. We had workshop days, during which we worked on the cars. Again, it was clear that Max understood this well and was used to helping his team. But it also became clear how little I knew about it.'

Max's first podium in a single-seater competition came in the first Palm Beach race on 4th February 2014, when he finished second to Antonio Fuoco. The Dutch teenager was so grateful that he gifted his glass trophy to his Prema Power team, signed and dedicated to the engineers who prepared his car. A week earlier, in the second race of the opening weekend at Sebring, he had damaged his car after locking up under braking and hitting the car in front of him. Despite having little time to repair the damage before the weekend's third race, the team's two mechanics nevertheless got the job done and Max was able to compete.

His mechanics greatly appreciated his gift of that second-place trophy at Palm Beach. After all, the first trophy won in a single-seater deserves a special place in any racer's trophy cabinet.

'You could tell from that how well adjusted he is,' observes Will Buxton. 'That trophy was his first in a single-seater. That does mean something, normally, no matter how many you win later. That first one, it's of great emotional value. And Max gave it to the mechanics.'

A day later Max scored his first victory. 'I'm keeping this one,' he said as he stepped off the rostrum.

Max won two races in the Florida Winter Series, at Palm Beach on 5th February and at Homestead on 19th February. He scored three fastest laps and three pole positions. He finished third in the final standings.

The Tatuus Formula Abarth cars in this one-make series were officially identical but some observers wondered if the Ferrari Driver Academy's youngsters were occasionally favoured. Jos Verstappen, indeed, noticed differences in engine exhaust that suggested a higher state of tune. Perhaps Max wasn't supposed to steal the show.

'Well, the boys of the junior team at Ferrari had to win of course,' recalls

Dennis van de Laar and Max pose for the photographer at
Hockenheim in May 2014.

Dennis van de Laar. 'Every weekend we had a different engineer, a different team-mate, a different chassis. That's a bit messy — and I did notice some differences between the cars. Ferrari wanted the series to be a success, but with their own drivers. No outsiders. It remains a bit of speculation, but politics did play a role.

'On the other hand, I was there to learn, and I think that was true for all the guys. And it was great to have an opportunity to race in the winter, when there's no motorsport back home. If you want to improve, you have to keep racing, but normally you can't do much of that between September and April.'

Testing in motor racing is also subject to restrictions, with Formula 3, for example, having only six private test days and six collective test days. Therefore, the opportunities to develop driving talent are quite restricted, other than the racing itself.

'This is a difficult aspect of motorsport,' says van de Laar. 'If you want to train or test, it's a huge logistical operation, with a team, a truck, a racing car and a track — all very expensive. But the FIA no longer allows that. It's different from football, where you can take a ball, find a field and get going. The same applies to tennis, athletics, you name it. Mechanical sports have this additional handicap in that respect. If you want to be good, you have to drive, drive and drive again — but that's no longer possible.'

Going back in time, Huub Rothengatter took that approach so seriously that even a broken back didn't stop him: on one occasion he drove a Formula Ford at Zandvoort while in a plaster cast, just to be able to rack up the laps. Jos Verstappen even travelled to the other end of the world, New Zealand, to race in the winter in Formula Pacific. That was also the idea behind the Florida Winter Series but it proved to be a one-off: the 2014 series was not only the first but also proved to be the last.

For Max, the end of the Florida Winter Series marked the start of a new adventure. As for Dennis van de Laar, he was gradually forced to face facts and recognise that he just wasn't quite good enough. After a season in the FIA European Formula 3 Championship, he decided to call it a day at the end of 2014.

'The fact that Max showed up and was immediately the fastest must have been sobering,' concludes Will Buxton. 'That's such a defining moment in your life. You manage to score the most beautiful girl in the class and then suddenly a new kid comes along and snatches her. There's only one conclusion after that. OK, I can never win this. I'm off.'

CHAPTER 9
FORMULA 3 SENSATION

Max's time in karting was over. He had won everything there was to win and now it was time to move to single-seater racing. The choice now before him would be decisive for his career. Even though Formula 3 seemed the obvious route, it wasn't as simple as that.

The world of high-level motorsport is all about money. The next step in Max's career simply had to be paid for, as the racing teams in these classes need financial contributions from their drivers in order to operate. The sums of money involved are substantial. To join a top team in European Formula 3, a driver not only has to be fast but also has to pay around 750,000 Euros. Even a driver as abundantly talented as Max Verstappen — everyone agreed on that — couldn't escape this unwritten law of motorsport, not even when driving for Frits van Amersfoort.

Van Amersfoort Racing (VAR) has been operational since 1975 and became involved in Formula 3 in 1997. Its owner attracts young drivers who hope to make the step to the big racing leagues through him. He has seen them come and go, in all shapes and sizes. From Mick Schumacher, son of Michael, to Jos, Max, and many others who have become Dutch cult racers. Jos himself began his single-seater career with van Amersfoort in Formula Opel Lotus in 1992 and became Benelux champion.

Van Amersfoort had been going through a lean period in the lead-up to the 2014 season but that year he was able to put his racing team back on the map. Formula 3, a class with only limited appeal to the general public, wasn't thriving at that time. When Max won the Masters at Zandvoort in July 2014, the grandstands and dunes were almost empty. Yet two years later, in June 2016, a demonstration run during the *Familie Race Dagen* (Family Race Days) event at Zandvoort caused chaos on the roads leading to the circuit. Track owner Prince Bernhard van Oranje Jr was delighted to see that motorsport was once again alive and well in the Netherlands.

VAR is based in the city of Zeewolde, in premises formerly occupied by sports car manufacturer Spyker, which experienced a single tumultuous year in Formula 1 in 2007, following which the team was sold and renamed Force India. When I visited, on the eve of a new season, the company was buzzing with activity. Employees walked in and out of the boss's refurbished office, which overlooks the workshop that used to house Spykers. Now it contains Formula 3 and Formula 4 cars in various stages of construction. In and around the building, the Spyker memories are unmistakable. In the car park, for example, there were still some trucks bearing the branding of the former racing team.

Frits van Amersfoort quietly plays an important background role on the Dutch motorsport scene. Now in his 60s, he has accumulated huge experience and been through all sorts of ups and downs. His team has evolved into a leading training academy for young drivers. He enjoys the work, which offers new challenges every season.

One of those challenges is the people who don't pay, usually parents claiming that their son didn't have 'the right equipment'. Motorsport can be an arena for excuses.

'In tennis it's easy,' says van Amersfoort. 'If you don't win, you can hardly blame your racket. With football it's also obvious. If you drive a racing car, all sorts of excuses can be made. These are then passed on to the team, or the engineer.'

As he talks, his curly grey hair dances wildly around his temples. He's smartly turned out, wearing a black polo shirt with his racing team's emblem embroidered in white on the chest.

'This is no ordinary company,' van Amersfoort explains enthusiastically. 'This is a racing team, where it's all about performance. There's always pressure. If not for the performance, then for the money.

Financial pressures have been alleviated in recent years because the arrival of a big investor has given the racing stable a new level of financial security.

Frits van Amersfoort — the man who ran Max Verstappen's
eye-opening Formula 3 campaign in 2014.

This investor, according to van Amersfoort, prefers to stay in the background. The relationship started with a cup of coffee on a beautiful autumn afternoon in the Austrian skiing resort of Söll. That popular adage — 'It's who you know, not what you know' — certainly applies in motorsport.

'There's a club of people in racing with whom you click,' says van Amersfoort. 'People who aren't in it for the money but through passion for the sport. Gerhard Berger is such a person. And Franz Tost [current boss of Scuderia AlphaTauri, formerly known as Toro Rosso]. And Huub Rothengatter. Contemporaries who feel the same way as I do. A few years ago Gerhard asked me if I was still managing to earn money with my Formula 3 team, to which I replied that I was just about making ends meet but that was all.'

In 2014, Berger, as President of the FIA's Single Seater Commission, wielded a new broom in Formula 3. The German and French championships disappeared and were replaced by a European championship, which would be larger, more prestigious, more expensive and more international. Van Amersfoort switched — 'with a lot of pulling and pushing' — from the German championship to the new European one.

A year later, he received a phone call from Berger. What were his thoughts about the new European series? This was at around the time when billionaire Lawrence Stroll, former owner of the Tommy Hilfiger brand, had just invested heavily in the rival Prema team, for which his son Lance drove. Big money was arriving in Formula 3.

'Formula 3, like football, was becoming more and more the plaything of billionaires,' says van Amersfoort. 'You can think what you want about that, but it's the reality.'

Max Verstappen's 2014 season with Van Amersfoort Racing left an indelible mark. Thanks to his success, VAR was on the up again. Within two years, the team was racing around Europe with a fleet of eight cars in FIA-sanctioned championships — four in Formula 3 and four in Formula 4. The operation grew quickly, to the point where it was employing 40 people.

One of VAR's Formula 4 drivers in 2015 was 16-year-old Mick Schumacher. That's a name that rings a bell. The son of the seven-times German Formula 1 World Champion ended up with a Dutch team not only because he wanted less attention from the German media, which had been stalking the Schumacher family since Michael's skiing accident in December 2013, but also because Max had achieved so much the previous year. Nevertheless, the younger Schumacher's arrival did confront VAR with the new experience of dealing with tabloid newspapers: the contract was full of clauses to protect the youngster — no photos, no interviews, media contact through the family only. 'At one point photographers were hiding in the bushes in front of our premises.'

Mick Schumacher drove one season in Formula 4 for VAR, giving the team proprietor enlightening insights into how talent works.

'Mick couldn't stand in Max's shadow,' van Amersfoort explains. 'Schumacher Jr isn't untalented. He can work very hard, just as Michael did. He also has that little bit of Schumacher luck and he has the name. With those things, you can go far, to Formula 1. He's a nice kid, but without the name he would probably have gone unnoticed. Mick also comes from a racing background and probably has his father's racing genes, but on the other hand he looks a lot like his mother. This is also the case with Max, but Sophie [his mother] has just as many racing genes as Jos.

'Mick was also raised very differently. He was never tutored by Michael but went karting because he liked it. Max has been drilled by Jos and you can see that now. Max's talent has been developed rigorously, rather like Andre Agassi or Richard Krajicek in tennis. They were locked up on the tennis court and relentlessly drilled. No-one had to force Max, because he always wanted to drive anyway.

'Mick eventually came to us after winning a simulator competition. He did a simulator test with us and we were enthusiastic about it.'

The young German's arrival took some getting used to, especially as VAR still had to recover from the previous year's rollercoaster ride with its new Dutch talent.

'Max hit the ground running on his very first day of testing in the Czech Republic,' recalls van Amersfoort. 'It was unbelievable. I've been around for a long time but I'd never experienced anything like it. He sat down in that car for the first time and immediately he was incredibly quick. He also continued to develop all year.

'In the long history of VAR we've never had such a talent. Nobody can match him. That's the truth. It wasn't fair to compare him with Senna, which everyone was starting to do, because that was a different era — just as you couldn't compare Senna with Fangio. I've seen young guys of all shapes and sizes come along since 1975, so I think I have some insight.'

When 16-year-old Max Verstappen arrived at VAR for the first time, it was like *déjà vu* for Frits van Amersfoort. Jos had joined the team when he was 19, in 1992, and already knew how to race. The boy was a young version of Jos, but already complete. Perfectly schooled in racing, bursting with talent and extremely eager to learn. A racing machine with a winner's mentality. Most of the work had already been done and that just continued with Jos in 2014. That close bond, that togetherness, created on the kart track and within the family simply continued in Formula 3.

A father/son relationship, judges van Amersfoort, works better in motorsport than in almost any other area of sport.

'It's inevitable that any youngster will make mistakes. When you're on your own, you have to make the mistakes in order to learn from them. A racing father, however, can protect his child from making those mistakes — and the child listens.

'At the end of the day, the Verstappens regard losing as unacceptable. That's my firm belief. But in professional motorsport you have to be able to lose, otherwise you become a burden to the team. Max is better at that than Jos — and he has more charm. When I watch these two now I get the impression that it's Jos who's now learning from Max.'

At the end of September 2013, when Max became karting world champion in the KZ class, the choice about his next step had to be made. Was it to be Formula Renault, an accepted 'entry-level' series in motor racing, or Formula 3, a somewhat more advanced category? Max's two mentors, his father and Huub Rothengatter, couldn't agree which route to take.

'Jos thought it best to go for Formula Renault, but Huub thought Formula 3 was a much better idea — and I fully agreed. Formula 3 was, and is, a serious competition run under the official rules of the World Motor Sport Council. It's the best environment for a young driver.'

Formula 3 offered stronger foundations for making further progress up the motorsport ladder. Although everyone used the same basic design of car from Italian constructor Dallara, the various teams could prepare the cars in their own way, with their own engineers and mechanics. There was a choice of 2-litre engines: VAR went for Volkswagen but there was a Mercedes alternative. In addition, tyres — supplied at the time by Hankook — played a significant part in the picture.

'It was clear to me that Max could make much better use of his talent in Formula 3. Formula Renault is more a kind of kit car, a compromise car. In

Young Max, still just a boy of 16, won 10 Formula 3 races in 2014, including two consecutive hat tricks.

Pumping a fist in the air, Max takes his first Formula 3 win,
at Hockenheim in May 2014.

Formula 3 things are more honest and the competition is closer to Formula 1.

'Max went testing everywhere at that time. He was outstanding in tests in Formula Renault. Often you see that guys who switch from karting to Formula Renault encounter problems, because they're very different disciplines. But with Max it was so obvious at the first test how good he already was. You didn't need to be psychic to see that. When a boy like that is fastest on at least 10 of the 14 test days in which he took part, in a field of 20 or so participants, that says something. If he could drive that fast in Formula Renault, Formula 3 wouldn't be a problem either.'

It was immediately obvious that the choice of Formula 3 with VAR was the right one for everyone concerned. It all worked smoothly: Max was fast, Jos gave instructions and Frits kept an eye on the big picture.

'After the first day it was already clear that it looked good. Max immediately had a good relationship with the car. He said he could do much more with it than with a Formula Renault. The first official test in Budapest put an end to all uncertainty. There were 27 other drivers and they all ended up behind him. If there were any doubts about whether Formula 3 was the right choice, they disappeared on that first day.

'Max then spent the whole season taunting the entire competition. I can't look into the minds of the other drivers, but it must have been frustrating. He may have had some less good races, but overall it was clear. Max was the boss.'

On 4th May, he won his first Formula 3 race, at Hockenheim, Germany. Nine more victories followed. In the final standings, he finished third, largely because of an untimely engine blow-up. He won more races than champion Esteban Ocon and runner-up Tom Blomqvist.

He scored two improbable hat-tricks, winning all three races at the Spa and Norisring rounds. These were the performances that caught the attention of Helmut Marko. Max stunned not only Red Bull's senior expert but also racing fans and rivals by producing a level of driving commitment unheard of in Formula 3, a category in which races often became uneventful parades.

Perhaps the best example of this came after that engine blow-up, which happened at the Nürburgring. It forced VAR to fit a new engine and that meant Max received a 10-place grid penalty for each of the next three races. In the first of these, still at the Nürburgring, he started 12th and finished third. In the last one, at Imola, he qualified on pole but dropped to 11th on the grid, from where he again climbed through the field to finish second.

At the Norisring, where he leads the field into the first hairpin, Max scored
the second of his two Formula 3 hat-tricks. Red Bull's Helmut Marko
watched the youngster dominate that weekend.

'Overtaking virtually the whole field like that is almost unheard of in Formula 3,' says van Amersfoort. 'These cars all go the same speed and the drivers aren't that far apart. Except if you have one of Max's calibre, especially at a nice track like Imola, which is relatively short and twisty. Then he can excel. Jos's big breakthrough in Formula Opel Lotus was at Zolder, another track where the driver can make a difference. On tracks like that the Verstappens can show they're better than the rest.'

As team boss, van Amersfoort can analyse exactly where a driver's strengths lie and how one distinguishes himself from others.

'After the year with Max, we went to test at Silverstone with our next team, in godforsaken cold weather in April. I tested three drivers. One of them, Charles Leclerc, was really good. So he collected the data that the others could use. But the next day the weather was different. It was even colder and the wind had changed direction. Leclerc adapted. The other guys followed up on the information from him and were thus slower — because the conditions had changed. The best drivers anticipate this.

'Max is such a driver. He can react to changing circumstances with lightning speed. He also knows exactly where he can gain time. Three-quarters of Max's brain is occupied with keeping the car on the track and he still has a quarter available to think about how that actually works. Many drivers never talk to their engineers when driving through corners, because they need to keep their attention on the job in hand, but Max does. Most drivers, especially the young guys who raced with me, need 100 percent to keep that thing on the track. So they have nothing left to know how to act. Max does.

'There was a kind of natural order to things. Jos analysed the circuit, Max started driving, encountered problems along the way and they had to be solved. Jos did that. Max listened, gave his opinion every now and then, but the conversation was mostly between Jos and Max's engineer. Max put his findings into practice on the track. Once in a while Max had his own ideas, but it was Jos who pushed his opinion on what the set-up of the car should be.'

One other element of Max's season with Frits van Amersfoort was that it brought an end to the long association between the Verstappens and Huub Rothengatter. It was a bond that seemed almost impossible to break, but that's what happened. Huub had a big disagreement with Jos and went his own way.

Mission accomplished: Jos, Max and Frits at the Macau Grand Prix at the
end of the 2014 season. Here Max's Van Amersfoort Racing Dallara was
turned out in Red Bull colours — a portent of things to come.

Huub and Frits have known each other for a very long time, right back to 1975. During the break-up, van Amersfoort had to stand on the sidelines but he felt some of the pain that Rothengatter must have felt.

'Huub was the first person to appreciate Max's talent. It still affects him emotionally when he thinks back to little Max's karting world title. Huub was euphoric at the time. It means a lot to him that it happened like that. That Rothengatter may be a stubborn bastard from time to time, but he does have a heart for motorsport and an eye for talent. The argument between those two should have been settled.'

That has never happened. The Verstappens and their mentor no longer speak to each other.

This is despite Rothengatter's very significant role in two of Max's most important career steps — the idea of going to the Florida Winter Series and then doing the Formula 3 season with Van Amersfoort Racing.

'Although he was the best driver in Florida,' says van Amersfoort, 'sometimes he wasn't allowed to win. He didn't get the best equipment or the best engineer. That made Huub realise that Max wouldn't be best placed in one of those one-make series, where they all drive the same car. When they came back from America, they started talking to me. It was a done deal.

'I have to say that Huub played a very important role during this period. He not only paid for the seat in Florida. After that, on the day we signed our contracts, Huub also provided a substantial part of the budget.'

The Verstappen/Rothengatter separation ultimately boils down to clashing personalities.

'Huub is a Rothengatter and Jos is a Verstappen. They can both be quite assertive and have difficulty admitting anything. It's no secret to say there was a bit of a row. I have experienced that too. At the Formula 3 race in Macau, the engineer was sacked by Jos. That's his character: he goes to the edge of what's permissible, but sometimes also over that edge.

'You're in a branch of sport where you're pushed to the limit. If you get into a fight, then you fight it out. But then you get back up, shake hands and carry on. That's the only way to grow in life. Drivers who always act like "yes men" won't get very far. It's a sport that demands 100 percent from you — 100 percent focus. If things happen that you feel are caused by someone else, then yes, it can be a trigger.

'Jos came from a simple background and also has an incredible obsession with winning. I think this character trait has determined his fate. Especially in the first year at Benetton, with Michael Schumacher. It was clear beforehand that he had to play second fiddle in that team. But it wasn't as easy as it seems now. Jos couldn't accept it. He couldn't accept that Michael was faster. If he'd understood that a bit better, I think his career would have gone very differently.

'Huub talked a lot to him about this, but to no avail.'

CHAPTER 10
INTERMEZZO

'**M**ax is a boy who's not afraid to be 18.' Those are the words of Johan Cruyff after meeting Max Verstappen at the Circuit de Catalunya. Remembering the occasion, Max almost cracks emotionally. The spontaneous encounter on 2nd March 2016 came to stand in sad perspective when Cruyff's sudden death just a few weeks later shocked the world. Asked about his reaction to the unexpected passing of the football legend, the teenager could hardly control his emotions and said that he was enormously proud to have met the Dutch folk hero. Here's a reconstruction of that remarkable meeting between two like-minded sportsmen.

Formula 1 was awakening from winter slumber when that casual meeting took place at a test session before the new season. At the Circuit de Catalunya, near Barcelona, the collective roar of Formula 1 engines was being heard once again. After the three-month pause following the end of the previous season, the teams were eager to run their latest cars. If anything, the sense of anticipation was even stronger than in previous years because the FIA had decided that teams would be limited to eight pre-season test days in 2016. The aim was to try to reduce some of the advantage enjoyed by the wealthier teams and contain the widening gap between the frontrunners and backmarkers.

This annual ritual of pre-season testing is always watched with great curiosity by the motorsport world. It's a moment that drivers, teams, fans and media have awaited with longing. The atmosphere in the bright spring sunshine seems relaxed but beneath this outward calm simmers anticipation. After months of work by hundreds of team personnel, the cars are ready for action.

For the drivers, too, the long wait comes to an end. The last Grand Prix of 2015, held in Abu Dhabi on 29th November, had been won by Mercedes driver Nico Rosberg. Thereafter, silence took over. The numerous Formula 1 websites quietened down, news became scarce, engines became dormant, and drivers disappeared from the spotlight to spend time with families and friends. But like the summer break in football, Formula 1's winter break is just the lull before the storm.

The atmosphere at Catalunya seems so relaxed that an outsider could easily fail to register the importance of it all. There's a lot of waiting for everyone except the engineers and data gatherers. While enormous amounts of data are processed in the pits, drivers and journalists have nothing much else to do other than wait. It can be a bit monotonous.

Then Johan Cruyff appears in the paddock. His arrival dispels the ennui and causes almost feverish excitement. He's dressed inconspicuously, wearing sunglasses and a black winter coat that hangs half open, enabling him to put his hands in his trouser pockets. The greyish hair around his temples appears thinner and his face looks a little fuller. To those who know what he has been through, he seems fitter.

This is remarkable, given that he was diagnosed with lung cancer only five months earlier, in October 2015. Since then he has endured intensive medical treatment, including five sessions of chemotherapy. But his fighting spirit is unbroken, as this memorable day in Spain proves. The answers he provides about the disease to the gathered journalists are sincere: 'It's half-time and I'm leading 2–0.'

Questions about his health, although uncomfortable, are unavoidable. Cruyff is a Dutch hero thrown in at the deep end, a man who's very much part of the national identity. The fans in his home country are worried. When the news broke that he was ill, all football stadiums in the Netherlands held a minute's silence. Seemingly, on this sunny day at Catalunya, his very presence somewhat reduces the uncertainties. His appearance and his willingness to talk to journalists are reasons for optimism.

It's no coincidence that he has travelled to the racetrack from his home nearby in Barcelona. As a sports enthusiast, he keeps an eye on all Dutch talent, not just footballers. He admires the runner Dafne Schippers as well as the young man he has come to meet here — Max Verstappen.

Cruyff doesn't differentiate between performance in motorsport compared with other sports. As he tells the media, he knows perfectly well how to be at the top of a sport that's 'not practised in a backyard for a couple of hundred spectators, but rather is played in an international arena'.

As an elite footballer, accomplished coach and global citizen recognised everywhere, he carries the pressure that comes with it very lightly. That's a trait that has also come to characterise Max during his début year in Formula 1. Cruyff articulates his opinions about the young Dutch racer like one of his inimitable dribbling runs. One short sentence in particular is noted eagerly.

'Max is a boy who's not afraid to be 18.'

In just a few minutes, that citation has been circulated across the internet.

In the pits of Max's team, Toro Rosso, three great sportsmen chat just like friends who meet regularly. Johan Cruyff (68), Jos Verstappen (43) and Max Verstappen (18) — their differences in age dissolve on the common topic of global top-level sport.

Cruyff momentarily draws media attention away from Max. Journalists want to know what the football phenomenon thinks about motorsport. Cruyff, who's becoming acquainted with Formula 1 for the first time, is astonished, in particular by the high level of professionalism and extraordinary attention to detail.

Jos explains some of this detail while Cruyff closely inspects the Toro Rosso's front wing. This intricate assembly is just a small part of a larger whole representing the entire technology of the car. Cruyff listens with amazement. The older Verstappen informs him that eight people worked on this wing for two weeks, and that its total cost is comparable to that of a complete Audi TT RS Roadster or a Range Rover Sport. Furthermore, a new layer has been added to the wing this season, a result of yet more highly scientific aerodynamic research. Perfection is expressed in every single square millimetre, reflects Cruyff, immediately drawing a parallel with football.

'So for each part there's a specialist? Football can certainly learn from this.'

A journalist asks if the young Max reminds him of a young Johan. This comparison had been made earlier by former Formula 1 driver Michael Bleekemolen. Max is an attacker by nature, as Cruyff was. Throughout his childhood, all his time went into karting. Playing football is also all that Johan did. Like Max, Johan burst through to the top level at a very young age, débuting for Ajax as a 16-year-old, and soon after playing in a championship-winning team.

Dutch sporting icons: Max Verstappen and Johan Cruyff
at their meeting on 2nd March 2016.

Johan Cruyff in his prime, during the World Cup quarter-final of 1974 against Argentina, when he scored two of the goals in the Dutch national team's 4–0 victory.

So, there are parallels. But, adds Cruyff, Max has one huge advantage — his father.

'He's the best teacher, someone Max can fully rely on and who possesses extensive knowledge of Formula 1. There's no better adviser.'

Cruyff's own father, Manus, died when Johan was just 12. Later, Johan benefited greatly from input from his father-in-law, Cor Coster, who got him up to speed with the business side of football. But Coster wasn't a football player. Jos was a Formula 1 driver. He knows exactly how it works, in all its sporting, financial and political aspects.

Fascinating dialogue develops throughout the morning between the football hero and the Formula 1 father and son. Boundaries between the two disciplines fade. Essentially, they're the same, Cruyff realises. Max talks about reaction training as part of a comprehensive physical training regime followed by drivers. The teenager demonstrates how he's able to tick 65 randomly generated squares on a digital touchscreen within 30 seconds. The idea behind this exercise is to enhance the ability to assess the view ahead of the car. Max instructs: 'It's a matter of bending your knees while looking straight ahead and in meantime taking care of the lights on the screen with both hands.'

Cruyff immediately sees similarities with football. Gesturing with his hands to strengthen his argument, he declares: 'This is the same with football. When you're in possession of the ball, you have to look over it to keep an overview. While dribbling, I was still able to quickly oversee everything on the pitch. So, it isn't only about pace on the pitch but also in the mind.'

Max then takes over, referring to new regulations for 2016 banning intercom communication with the pits. The sheer quantity of tasks for the driver, controlled by more than 20 buttons on the steering wheel, and operated at speeds up to 200mph, is dazzling. 'That's what reaction training is useful for. I have to look over the steering wheel constantly, process the information swiftly, and make decisions.'

Speed of thought in a racing car or on a football pitch — the theme offers both Johan and Max various comparable points to discuss. For Cruyff, who's relatively unfamiliar with motorsport, it all points to the same thing. A great talent makes all necessary decisions at the right moment.

The football legend refers to the incident in Singapore in 2015. Towards the end of the race, Verstappen was told over the on-board radio that he had to let Carlos Sainz Jr, his supposedly quicker team-mate, overtake him: 'Max, you need to let him go. Swap please.' The teenager gave his stone-cold response immediately: 'No!'

Cruyff approved of that rebellious streak.

It reminded him of a question in 2008 from Pep Guardiola, one of his protégés, after the Spaniard had been approached to succeed Frank Rijkaard as manager of Barcelona. Guardiola asked Cruyff, who himself had managed Barcelona in the period 1988–96, if he should accept the offer. Cruyff replied: 'Only if you're prepared to tell the president to keep out of the locker room. He has no business there. But you can only get away with it if you're right.'

And, in that way, Cruyff confirmed to Max that he, too, had been right when racing against Carlos Sainz Jr in Singapore.

Max is keen on playing football. He's also a Barcelona fan and follows the team as much as possible. Still, as he confessed to Cruyff, he quickly discovered that there were better footballers than him. That confession prompted another one.

'The first time I drove a kart, it felt like I was driving amazingly, so close to the ground, helmet on, and pedal to the metal. Until a driver approached me and said: "I'm quicker than this while in reverse."'

With unconcealed pride, Max tweeted later that afternoon: 'Fantastic to meet the legendary sportsman Johan Cruyff.'

And Cruyff replied: 'It's been nice to meet a great talent and fellow Dutchman.'

Just over three weeks later, on 24th March 2016, the great Johan Cruyff passed away.

PART 2
FORMULA 1

CHAPTER 11
CARNAGE AT COPSE

A s I was reaching this second half of my story about Max Verstappen's road to Formula 1 greatness, a hair-raising incident took place at one of Silverstone's famous corners. On 18th July 2021, at just after two o'clock in the afternoon on the first lap of the British Grand Prix, the left-front wheel of Lewis Hamilton's Mercedes hits the right-rear wheel of Max Verstappen's Red Bull while they travel at a speed of around 180mph into Copse Corner. The consequences are dramatic. Although there's a large gravel run-off area to slow down a crashing car, the force with which the Red Bull RB16B hits the tyre wall is enormous. The car slams sideways and Max's body absorbs an impact of 51G. That's a blow of approximately 4,000kg, as if a bulldozer fell from the sky onto the driver's body. Not much is left of the car. Its carbon-fibre body has been crumpled like paper and the wheels are bent crookedly around the wreckage.

The instigator of all this, the reigning World Champion, races on and receives merely a 10-second penalty, which he brushes aside like a speck of dust on a shoulder of his race suit. He goes on to win the British Grand Prix in front of his home fans.

This outcome is infuriating for Red Bull and Max Verstappen, who has to be taken to a local hospital for a medical check-up while the race remains in progress. After the crash, he wriggles out of his car's cramped cockpit, shaken and dizzy, and struggles to climb out through the halo, the protective ring around the driver's seat. He has to be supported by marshals, who take him

Prelude to the collision: Lewis Hamilton and Max Verstappen take off side-by-side at the start of the 2021 British Grand Prix at Silverstone.

to an ambulance. It's a wonder that he can stand more or less on his own two feet, waving to the grandstands with his head bowed, to let the spectators know he's in reasonable shape. A crash of this magnitude could have been fatal a few years earlier.

'We almost lost one of the most talented drivers in modern racing history,' said three-times World Champion Sir Jackie Stewart. 'In my day, Max would not have survived. It was Lewis's fault, no doubt. The punishment he got for it was frankly ridiculous.'

We will return to this topic. Sir Jackie thinks that the balance between punishment and safety has been lost in today's Formula 1 and the matter merits more discussion. Especially as Max Verstappen belongs to a generation of drivers who think they're invulnerable and seem to take the risks of racing for granted. Injuries are mercifully scarce because the cars are super-safe and so are the circuits, with huge run-off areas and shock-absorbing barriers as at Silverstone's Copse Corner. Racing a modern Formula 1 car is so relatively safe that a driver appears to be able to withstand the force of 51G unscathed.

The Dutchman's physique had been put to the test before. One occasion was in Azerbaijan in 2021, after a tyre blow-out on the long straight at Baku. Another occurred in Monaco in 2015, when he crashed after clipping the back of Romain Grosjean's Haas car while overtaking it, going into a tyre wall head-on at a speed of about 75mph with an impact force of around 20G.

But Silverstone 2021 — that was the mother of all crashes. A normal individual would count his blessings after such an experience and send out a tweet from the hospital saying: 'Okay guys, that's it, I quit.' But drivers aren't ordinary people. Ross Brawn, former technical director at Ferrari and now Formula 1's overall technical supremo, knows drivers' attitudes like no other. After all, he was Michael Schumacher's boss in his rampant Ferrari years: 'Drivers would race with shopping trolleys across a car park if they met each other there.'

This is especially true for a descendant of Jos Verstappen. Max is ruthless when it comes to a battle on the track. The usual expression for it is 'death or glory' and the Dutch have their own version of this, *dood of gladiolen* ('death or gladioli'), used at cycling events, referring back to Roman times when a winning gladiator would be showered in gladioli flowers.

In motor racing, historically, the battles have been almost literally between life and death, especially between arch-rivals. History is littered with drivers who eliminated themselves rather than let a rival pass.

The crash at Silverstone's Copse Corner left Red Bull with a destroyed
car and Max Verstappen lucky to escape injury.

Think of Michael Schumacher. Controversy surrounded his 1994 world title after he deliberately punted Damon Hill off the track in Adelaide. A racing accident; it can happen. When he pulled the same trick on Jacques Villeneuve at Jerez in 1997 he didn't get away with it and was disqualified from the World Championship.

Legendary and ruthless were the battles between Brazilian phenomenon Ayrton Senna and French 'professor' Alain Prost, twice ending off the track in Japan, in 1989 and 1990. Racing accidents, both called them, but was that really the case? Or were they intentional?

The crash between Verstappen and Hamilton at Silverstone formed a demarcation line between two generations. The departing man, already 36 years old, who knows that it's almost over but presses on in his quest for yet more honours, and the coming man of 23, who's busy trying to vanquish the old champion and doesn't give up. It's hand-to-hand fighting... almost to the death. That's how it was at Copse Corner.

Analyse that duel, frame by frame. This wasn't even about deciding the world title. This was about who has the biggest dick, who can pee further. And who has the biggest heart. When it comes to Max, that heart is full of his father's DNA. Remember the words of Jos's former team boss: 'If he couldn't pass someone on the track, he might go over them if necessary.'

That uncompromising attitude is a trait of the son as well. Except that at Copse Corner the line between guilt and innocence is razor-thin. This is cutting-edge Formula 1, with an intensity to the jousting that fans around the world love. But where does fighting spirit end and recklessness begin? Perhaps it was a racing incident, but the jury still wants to send a signal that things cannot go on like this.

Formula 1 isn't a contact sport. Frame by frame, from every camera angle, the incident is reviewed. The verdict favours Verstappen, probably because the footage shows that he steered a fraction to the left just before the crash, to avoid a collision. The reigning World Champion may have been counting on his great rival of 2021 to hold back. After all, the race had hardly begun. Not even a lap had been completed. Hamilton misses the apex by a whisker, Max doesn't budge. The consequences are enormous.

The physical harm to the Red Bull driver is only slight, but the cost of damage to his car amounts to well over £1 million, in a season when a budget cap has been introduced for the first time in the history of the sport.

Welcome to the wonderful world of Formula 1 and the titanic showdown for a world title. The gloves are off after that incident at Copse Corner. No more Mr Nice Guy. From now on, diplomacy has gone. Max Verstappen and Red Bull are no longer runners-up, but dangerous opponents of Mercedes and Lewis Hamilton. Max Verstappen has become the only challenger to the World Champion, following in the footsteps of legendary predecessors who toppled kings and overthrew kingdoms.

As dramatic as it sounds, Silverstone on 18th July 2021 marked the end of an era.

And the beginning of a new one.

CHAPTER 12
THE FIRST WORDS

The media centre, Melbourne, Australia, 12th March 2015. It's the first Grand Prix of the year and as usual the room is filled to the brim with journalists. They're eager for information. The annual winter tests in Barcelona a few weeks earlier have been their only reference point for the new season's prospects, but that doesn't help them much. Those who were in Spain dutifully recorded what drivers, engineers and team bosses said, but knew that the prelude at the Circuit de Catalunya gives little indication of the true balance of power. No — that will emerge here in Australia. This is the real start to yet another season of Grand Prix racing that will separate the men from the boys.

Max Verstappen is still a boy. This stimulates the curiosity of the media. One Dutch journalist jokingly says he's still a *jambekkie* (best translated as 'wet-behind-the-ears kid'). There's a lot of scepticism across the Formula 1 community. Who's this guy from the Netherlands? Or, more harshly, who does this kid think he is? International journalists research his history and describe it to their readers, who irreverently distil it to the basics: Max is the son of Jos Verstappen, who crashed a lot... at 17, he's the youngest-ever participant in a Grand Prix... he drives for Red Bull's 'junior' team, Toro Rosso...

The young Dutchman is attending his first press conference of the year. He's part of a six-strong line-up of predators and prey. Lewis Hamilton's there, the untouchable World Champion; Sebastian Vettel, driving for Ferrari and the man expected to be the British driver's main challenger; Daniel Ricciardo, *numero uno* at Red Bull; plus Valtteri Bottas of Williams and Kevin Magnussen of McLaren, middle-ranking men.

The atmosphere during this presentation is fairly relaxed but also feels forced. The men behind the microphones look untouchable while sporting the distinct colours of their respective teams. They give obvious answers to obvious questions.

What could be going through Max's mind at that moment? He's the newcomer, surrounded by rivals and facing masses of journalists. Some want honest information, others hope for a controversial quote, if necessary extracted through biased questions to the protagonists. Most participants at the press conference know how it works. They talk a lot without saying anything. Tongue in cheek, to take the sting out of the conversation. A press conference is like a Formula 1 race. A small mistake can send you flying off. That's certainly the case with modern media, which rushes to serve readers, viewers and listeners worldwide at the speed of light.

Max calmly gazes into the room. He emits an authentic aura, has nothing to hide. That's more than enough for a 17-year-old. He doesn't have a big mouth, is careful not to say too many big words, and thus unintentionally and unconsciously charms the crowd represented by the media people sitting in front of him.

He looks relaxed behind the microphone. Next to him and in front of him are his fellow drivers, whom until recently he has admired from afar. In the audience are the journalists, mostly middle-aged men who are well versed in the business. The cameras are rolling and every word, facial expression and gesture is captured. When a driver moves, dozens of cameras click to record it, after which an editor can interpret it in an accompanying caption.

He looks wide-eyed and innocent. An expression of mild surprise flickers on his face in reaction to one reporter's question. He doesn't know the man. In fact he knows hardly anyone in the media. There are a few Dutch journalists in the room but they don't ask him anything. They prefer to question him later, separately. He's wary — and yet at the same time he isn't. While visibly at ease, he doesn't really know what to do with his posture. He watches and listens to the veteran drivers, who casually and routinely go through the motions of the press conference, with Hamilton and Vettel leading the way. Ricciardo smiles. Bottas seems uptight. Magnussen looks reserved and serious. These last two are Scandinavian, both very different from former World Champion

Australia 2015 — Max's first Formula 1 press conference. He sits at rear left alongside Valtteri Bottas and Kevin Magnussen, with Sebastian Vettel, Lewis Hamilton and Daniel Ricciardo in front

and fellow Viking Mika Häkkinen, who had an inexhaustible supply of dry humour at his disposal for these occasions.

Max, a novice in this situation, has to find a balance between self-confidence, strength, modesty, sincerity and political correctness. Moreover, he has to express himself in a language that isn't his own. He grew up amongst easy-going Limburg people for whom conviviality is natural. Conviviality doesn't exist in Formula 1.

Fortunately, he wasn't brought up in an easy-going household and that makes a difference. His father was always on top of things, keeping the pressure on. Later Max would say that he was never bothered by harsh criticism. After all, he was used to his father and Jos was sterner than the most severe critic. It would never get worse. Even when he'd won a race easily, practically with his eyes closed, his father had seen something wrong somewhere. 'How often have I heard that I was going to become a truck driver because I was so relaxed? Or that I was being called a lazy pig.'

No, it wouldn't get any worse than that. So, handling a press conference isn't a concern. Verstappen is the kind of guy who doesn't fuss about anything, especially not a question from some unfamiliar journalist. With an open mind and in flawless English, Max answers briefly and clearly.

At first, he sits there for a long time, disengaged. The men around him, led by two undisputed alphas, are given the floor first.

Then, after a long time, comes the first question for Max Verstappen. The first official question in an FIA press conference. The question is much longer than the answer.

'And finally, Max Verstappen. Welcome. The youngest Formula 1 driver ever at 17 years old. Are you ready?'

What the questioner expects as an answer is unclear. It's ceremonial theatre, devoid of content. Maybe if Max had been older and more experienced, he would have made a joke of it. 'No way, I'm only here to fill up the field... Of course I'm not ready. Are you crazy? I'm 17 years old. How ready can I be?... I'm very nervous and it's amazing that I'm here, among all these fantastic drivers... I haven't slept for the last few weeks... Just thinking about this moment made me sweat...'

Of course, he doesn't say any of those things. None of it would have been true anyway. Max Verstappen is 100 percent ready. He cannot wait for the lights to go out and take the first corner at Albert Park in the midst of his rivals and peers.

He says: 'I hope so! We'll see.'

These are the future World Champion's first words in the big league.

There's no applause, but the uttered sentences are obediently noted down and appear in the world's media a little later.

Lewis Hamilton is asked a question about Max and reacts endearingly. He cannot yet suspect that he's speaking about a future enemy.

'Lewis, any pearls of wisdom? You were five years older than Max, I think, when you made your début. Is that right? Twenty-two?

'Possibly. I've only just realised, I'm the oldest driver here, the first time. I've kind of only just realised it. Jeez. [To Max] You were born in '97?

'Yup.'

'Jeez. I signed my first contract with McLaren in '97. Bloody 'ell. I don't really have any words of wisdom for you.'

Sebastian Vettel calmly adds: 'I think that despite the fact that he's still young, I think he has a lot of experience, he's quick, otherwise he wouldn't be here, so I don't think he needs much advice. Take it easy, maybe.'

Another reporter asks if he's impressed with his new life as a 17-year-old, flying around the world, amongst guys he looks up to. 'How is it for you?'

Max replies, with eyes that ask as much as they tell.

'Well, to be honest, since I was younger, I've never seen anything else because my Dad was doing it, I basically grew up into it. For me, it doesn't feel like anything new, I just deal with it.'

The teenager's words aren't universally welcomed. Some find them arrogant, spoken by a brat who should remain more modest for a while.

Journalist Peter Windsor: 'That's right. Some people thought Max was arrogant and bossy. Maybe it seemed that way, but I didn't experience it that way. He had self-confidence, of course. If you don't have confidence, you don't belong in this sport.'

As time passes, as Grands Prix come and go, it becomes apparent that Max Verstappen doesn't really like these compulsory media appearances, but they're part of the circus and part of his job. Later, when his spotless record occasionally gets tarnished, he sometimes takes a hard line.

Jos Verstappen didn't much like the media either. In the rather different world of his time, he could readily dismiss an annoying journalist with words such as 'Get lost' or 'What nonsense are you talking, man'. Political correctness isn't for the Verstappens. Things were much less 'official' then. There weren't cameras at every angle and press conferences weren't cast in such an oppressive format. That gave more freedom to say something worthwhile, more than is possible now. Not that Jos has had any influence on Max's media performances — actually he couldn't care less. For Verstappen senior the media were a necessary evil and for junior the same applies.

These days Max talks like he races. Correctly where possible, hard if necessary. In Canada in 2018, a British journalist asked him why he was having so many accidents. The Dutchman didn't mince his words.

'I don't know. And, like I said in the beginning of this press conference, I get really tired of all the questions, so... yeah... I think if I get a few more I'll head-butt someone.'

That, too, was how he reacted after the Copse Corner carnage at Silverstone in 2021, at the first press conference in Hungary a fortnight later. On that Thursday — the day on which drivers have no track commitments but plenty of media responsibilities — he was still answering questions about the incident, seemingly with patience. For the previous 10 days the incident had been analysed exhaustively. Of course, journalists had questions and now, with Max in front of them, they were curious to get first-hand answers.

But when a questioner returned to the topic at the subsequent press conference, after qualifying, the Dutchman had had enough. In no uncertain terms, he spoke his mind.

'Can we just already stop about this because it's... we've had so many fucking questions about this. It's just ridiculous, honestly. Honestly, the whole Thursday we've been answering this stupid crap all the time. So can we just stop about it please?'

That was too direct for many. The Dutch aren't known for their politeness. The FIA press officer apologised on Max's behalf. But that didn't go down well either.

'I don't want you to apologise on my behalf,' Max snapped as he passed.

The Dutch are generally quite outspoken in the eyes of the more reserved international community. With the Verstappens this is especially true.

Peter Windsor: 'I think it's very difficult for anyone to imagine what it's like to be the centre of attention all the time and how to behave. Most of the questions journalists ask are incredibly stupid and most of the topics they want to talk about are completely irrelevant to the driver, because they're not about the sport at all.'

Back in Australia in 2015, the controversies all lay in the future. A fresh face joins the seasoned campaigners and effortlessly steals the hearts of many. Not just of inveterate Formula 1 followers, but women, young and old, and boys and girls. Peter Windsor was immediately captivated by the unreconstructed Dutchman.

'The media ruins it for so many athletes and sports people. Max knows that, has known it from day one, and stays true to himself. And that works. My mother is 100 years old, but Max is her absolute favourite Formula 1 driver. She loves the way he is, the way he smiles, the answers he gives. She loves all aspects of his personality and if he doesn't win she's upset. One hundred, huh!

'Max is a lovely guy and I mean that sincerely. He loves his life and appreciates the privileges that come with it. He's a bit like Lewis, who also has his feet firmly on the ground, largely due to his disabled brother Nicholas. Lewis says he's happy with what he has and will never take advantage of it. Max has his family, who keep him humble. These are authentic people.'

Let's get out on the track at Melbourne. Max Verstappen is driving a Toro Rosso. He's under the guidance of team principal Franz Tost, who cannot believe his luck in having two young drivers of such calibre. The other Toro Rosso driver, Carlos Sainz Jr, another rookie, puts down a marker straight away. He qualifies better than Verstappen, even reaching Q3 with a neat eighth place. Max 'only' manages to qualify 12th, which must be a disappointment. After all, a driver's first task is to beat his team-mate and that hasn't happened.

Excuses — mitigating circumstances like inexperience or an under-performing car — aren't appropriate. Max Verstappen has won everywhere, has always driven at the front. Now he's forced to race in midfield, surrounded by drivers whom he's convinced he would beat in like-for-like circumstances.

Patience is needed. His father Jos was impatient and that's why his Formula 1 début, at the 1994 Brazilian Grand Prix as Michael Schumacher's team-mate, went so wrong, resulting in a huge crash. It was Ferrari driver Eddie Irvine's fault but, as every driver knows, excuses don't count. Sainz Jr, who shares something of Jos's driving style according to some observers, also does better than Max in the race. The Spaniard finishes in the points, a magnificent ninth. Max drops out on lap 32 with engine trouble.

Some of the initial excitement has subsided. At home, in the Netherlands,

When Australian journalist Peter Windsor witnessed Max Verstappen
make his Formula 1 début in the 2015 Australian Grand Prix,
he was impressed with what he saw.

'scoreboard journalism' prevails and shoulders are shrugged. A new Verstappen has arrived and he's already out of contention in his first race. What's new?

It will never work out for him.

How wrong these pessimists were.

A phenomenon in the making. That's how you could describe Max Verstappen's first year in Formula 1. Too young to challenge the top dogs, but old enough to perform sensibly. Most other youngsters would still be pretty wild at 17, seeing errors and blunders as part of the learning curve.

There's no time for that in Formula 1. It's a ruthless arena. Had Max made serious mistakes in his first year, it would have been over and done with. Although he had the solid support of Red Bull's management, he couldn't afford youthful over-confidence. That can can cost millions in this sport — and endanger safety. What starts as firm belief in a driver's qualities can turn to scepticism and doubt within just a few races.

Father Jos experienced that personally. He too was warmly embraced and showered with praise only to wither away in the shadow of Michael Schumacher at Benetton halfway through the season. His career was over almost before it had started. He wasn't even allowed to finish that first season, forced to make way for Englishman Johnny Herbert.

Max had everything going for him when he entered Formula 1... but the unpredictable can still happen. Setbacks due to bad luck and unfortunate circumstances can mean that it's soon all over. There's a long list of one-hit wonders in Formula 1 history.

Franz Tost, his first team boss and close colleague of Red Bull adviser Helmut Marko, had seen Verstappen in action with Marko at the Norisring in 2014, the signature Formula 3 race at which Max had made such an indelible impression. That weekend he was two seconds per lap quicker than everyone else in difficult conditions. What's more, Norisring is a short track and those laps took only 50 seconds.

A question remained about that 2015 season. Why did Red Bull's management not immediately put Max in the senior team, where the drivers were three-times winner Daniel Ricciardo and new Toro Rosso graduate Daniil Kvyat, rather than wait until the following year? According to the hugely respected Peter Windsor, that would have been much better.

'If they'd shown even more confidence in the boy, all that time at Toro

Rosso wouldn't have been necessary. When he was put in the Red Bull in Barcelona over a year later, many so-called experts said they were taking a big risk. I would have taken him straight to the A-team. What risk would that have been? None. How good he would become was perhaps the risk, not his age. Look at other guys they've put in their cars. Scott Speed, for example. Give me a break. If all the fuss about Speed is recalled for a moment, Max was a no-brainer as far as I'm concerned.'

When Red Bull Racing set up its second-string Toro Rosso operation at the start of the 2006 season, Speed was one of its contracted test drivers and was put in the new team. The American's results were poor and halfway through the 2007 season, after 28 races, he was released from his contract and replaced by Sebastian Vettel. Speed disappeared from Formula 1. Vettel went on to win the World Championship four times.

With hindsight, everything is easier to judge, but Windsor, thanks to all his accumulated experience and technical knowledge of Formula 1, invariably knows what he's talking about. Especially when it comes to Max Verstappen. Windsor's truth doesn't lie in the media centre, where journalists feed each other, sometimes with useful information but mostly with speculation and backbiting. Windsor prefers not to watch a race on the screens in the media centre, but rather to go out to the track for good close-up views of real action. With over 50 years of experience in many areas of Formula 1, from journalism to team management, he can quickly recognise a driver's qualities.

At the different circuits around the world, Windsor takes up trackside positions that tell him the most. At Sepang in Malaysia, for example, he spectates at Turns Five and Six. In Barcelona, a key race for him, between Turns Two and Three. These are corners that for the untrained eye seem ordinary, like so many others during a season, but each has its own dynamics, and each lap has its own elements dictated by countless variables: weather, wind, tyre wear, track temperature, a car's decreasing weight as its fuel tank empties. It's like riding a motorcycle over a mountain pass, with hairpin bends all the way. It might look straightforward but no two bends are the same and each requires a different approach. It's the same on any racetrack.

'I sit at such corners,' says Windsor, 'because the TV cameras hardly ever film at a good angle. On some circuits it's difficult to find a good corner and in Melbourne that's particularly the case, so I didn't get a clear picture of him there. But I soon saw that Max has a level and a touch that are almost unmatched. Something you only see with the greatest. I only really noticed

Max's second Grand Prix, Sepang 2015, brought his first World Championship points. Here he duels with Red Bull's Daniel Ricciardo, his future team-mate.

that at Sepang and later in Barcelona. There you can really see the difference between the extremely good drivers and the rest.'

After Max's unspectacular first Formula 1 race in Melbourne, there was little cause for fuss, but that soon changed.

Windsor took his trackside seat at the next Grand Prix, in Malaysia, and followed the Dutchman closely, analysing steering movements, watching entries and exits, observing the differences between the drivers — and then seeing his findings confirmed. There at Sepang, in scorching heat and enervating humidity, where drivers lose litres through perspiration, the battle intensifies on numerous levels. Against the rivals, against the conditions, against the track, against the heat and against himself. On television, driving a Formula 1 racing car seems no more than that — driving a car. At least that's how it seems for the 17-year-old, who's completely in his element. Although Melbourne hadn't revealed much about the Dutchman, Sepang provided plenty of insight. This was perhaps the race at which Max Verstappen, the boy, became a man.

It was a brilliant performance. In finishing seventh, he even stayed ahead of the Red Bull A-team's two drivers. He became the youngest driver ever to score World Championship points, a record that will stand forever because 17-year-olds are no longer allowed to compete in Formula 1. And his driving style had an identity of its own. There, in Sepang, Max Verstappen showed that driver and car can be one. He drove with a level of intuition and feeling that few can match.

Max does everything, according to Peter Windsor, by feeling. His pressure on the brake pedal is never brute force. It's sometimes quite light, then, where necessary, a little harder. As has become apparent over the years, he rarely locks the wheels. As a result, his tyres often remain in better condition, without the 'flat spots' that adversely affect a car's handling. The Toro Rosso wasn't even one of the better cars and yet his relationship with it was already revealing itself.

'Just like Lewis, Max manipulates the car,' says Windsor. 'Only the very best do that. At the moment the only other drivers who do that are Charles [Leclerc], Lando [Norris] and George [Russell]. It's as if these guys are driving the cars with their fingertips. Everything is as light as a feather. On the telemetry you don't usually see big peaks or drops in performance. They're drivers who look ahead, who anticipate rather than react. See the difference between Pérez and Max, or between Bottas and Lewis. We can agree that they're all excellent drivers, otherwise you won't get very far. Many drivers react to the circumstances, brake late, or brake additionally in a corner, steer late, or early, and are usually guided by their attacking instincts.

'Max is an early braker. He brakes sooner than his team-mate in order to position himself better in the corner. Drivers like him absorb the track and aren't inclined to brake too late, such that they have to correct that in the corner. This is all in milliseconds, of course. They get their speed from stable steering and an incredible feeling on the brake pedal and steering wheel, so they come out of the corner at a higher speed than the late brakers. Most young drivers are used to braking as late as possible and think they're fast. But late braking isn't the answer, as Max proves.

'Most people don't understand that an early braker is faster. All the greats, past and present, have that characteristic. Jim Clark, Stirling Moss... Lewis, Charles. Problem is, you can't learn a driving style like that. You have to be born with it.'

But there's much more, and that has to do with the structure within Formula 1. The teams are so big, the data input so enormous, that the drivers are only a small part of the package. As the data is paramount, drivers can tend to hide behind it. If a car isn't fast enough in the corners, it can be due to numerous factors that also interact with each other through different forces. The truth tends to get buried under numbers.

With driver and car, it can be like chicken and egg. One driver asks for more downforce, the other thinks twice if an aerodynamic adjustment will solve a problem. Max Verstappen feels the car through his backside and optimises performance through his supreme driving skills.

'Besides,' adds Windsor, 'Red Bull doesn't tell him how to drive. They trust him completely and let him do his thing. That's the problem with lesser drivers. They ask for instructions from the team on how to drive. But that doesn't make for a better driver. In Max's case he solved it himself. He didn't need the technical discipline that Carlos Sainz Jr required because it came naturally to him. His teams gave him enough breathing space to do his own thing. Nobody had to tell him that at one point or another on the track he was braking too late or too early. He knew that himself.'

Back to Sepang, where Max Verstappen has shown what he can do. Back home in the Netherlands, people are slowly waking up, and the world is following suit. Motorsport fans are starting to believe in Max. The Dutch prodigy is becoming a reason to turn on the television and follow Formula 1.

CHAPTER 13
MONACO

The Monaco Grand Prix 2021. Max Verstappen is untouchable. Like a true champion, he dominates the entire weekend in the principality, where Formula 1 has returned after a year's absence due to Covid. Fastest in free practice. Impeccable and elusive during qualifying. And then race day: from pole position to chequered flag, leading every lap.

If this wasn't Monaco, it would be judged a very dull race. But Monaco has always been an enigma. Normally the narrow, winding streets are occupied by average road users, even if 'average' is hardly a word suited to life in a tax haven, and the uneven road surfaces are incredibly tricky for drivers of Formula 1 cars with rock-hard suspension. However, the tradition of glamour and glitz, the aura of the rich and famous, the spectacular harbour filled with lavish yachts, the corners with names that sound like motorsport poetry — all this is so evocative that a Formula 1 season without Monaco, as in 2020, is really only half a season.

The race itself is more or less an afterthought at a weekend where seeing and being seen in the paddock is at least as important. The race is usually predictable. The pole-sitter often wins. Overtaking is virtually impossible.

Watching Formula 1 at Monaco, however, is never uneventful because the devil is hidden in the detail. Over-confidence, misjudgement, a split-second loss of focus — all can have major consequences on this track and within seconds can turn a dull parade into pandemonium. This circuit is unforgiving. The narrow corners, surrounded by steel guardrails and tyre walls, and surfaced with bumpy tarmac, are as treacherous as thin ice. The circuit's hazards are conveniently forgotten by the outside world. The uninitiated just see the parade. But the knowledgeable fan sees a blood-curdling dance on a tightrope above a gaping abyss. Either way, winning at Monaco is one of the finest prizes in motorsport.

In 2021, Max Verstappen wrote history again. With his seemingly effortless victory, he looked like one of the greats of Formula 1, one of those who excel in Monaco. Ayrton Senna won here six times, Graham Hill and Michael Schumacher five, Alain Prost four. Behind them, Stirling Moss, Jackie Stewart and Nico Rosberg each won three times, and Lewis Hamilton's score is three as well.

Max's one win — so far — could have been more. But there again he was so young on his début at this track when he hit a tyre barrier for the first time. The spectacular accident in 2015 involving Romain Grosjean at Ste Dévote haunted him for a long time, because in the years that followed there was always disappointment.

That Grosjean incident reverberated around the Formula 1 circus, especially in media land. 'Told you so,' a number of press voices shouted. 'He's too young.' At the front of the pack delivering these blows was Jacques Villeneuve, 1997 World Champion and Formula 1 pundit.

'They jumped on the bandwagon *en masse*, judging Max to be too young, even though the accident really wasn't his fault,' says top journalist Peter Windsor, who remains indignant about it all. 'The crash was entirely Grosjean's fault. The data showed that he applied the brakes earlier on that lap than on previous laps.

'But apart from that, the way Max recovered in Canada [the next race] was impressive.'

That incident at Ste Dévote was almost heart-stopping. Mother Sophie, who must have seen it on television, would have been painfully reminded of the day her young son crashed his kart in her presence.

The near-catastrophe in Monaco occurred in the blink of an eye. The 17-year-old didn't actually do what's advised when a racing car crashes almost head-on — take his hands off the steering wheel to prevent worse potential injury. His father Jos had taught him that and all experienced Formula 1 drivers know to do it. But he wasn't yet an experienced Formula 1 driver. He had never endured a crash of this magnitude, one that could have broken his legs, so instead he was still hoping to steer the car even though it was completely out of control.

Michael Schumacher had a similar crash with his Ferrari at Silverstone in the 1999 British Grand Prix, at the fast Stowe corner, and broke his right leg in several places, forcing him to miss eight races. He judged this accident 'the worst of my career'. Miraculously, at Monaco in 2015, Max Verstappen escaped with no injuries. His 'yeah I'm all right' that came through the onboard radio was music to everyone's ears, especially his family.

According to British journalist David Tremayne, Verstappen showed his true character there: 'I was reminded of the days of Chris Amon with the Ensign when he crashed in Sweden in 1976 — it seems like an eternity ago now — when drivers could perish. For Amon, that was the reason to stop racing. There are a lot of drivers who are completely out of it after a serious accident. Max? You see him walking and think: this has done nothing to him. I think he has a very rational reasoning that these things come with the territory and you have to accept them when you're a driver.'

Max's close bond with his father also helped to put the crash quickly behind him.

Peter Windsor: 'Jos and Max went out for dinner together on the Tuesday, then Max got into a kart and drove for a full day in the rain to get back to basics. And that paid off at the next Grand Prix when he drove well, didn't do anything crazy and finished 12th in the Toro Rosso. Then I thought: wow, this guy really has his feet on the ground. He's doing exactly what he needs to do under these circumstances.'

Max Verstappen continued to have a difficult relationship with the Monaco Grand Prix, a race that gives an ordinary winner immortal status. In 2019, he drove helplessly behind Lewis Hamilton, desperately looking for moments to pass but not finding them. He then resigned himself to the situation, despite the frustrations. His attempts to overtake Hamilton remained considerate and without undue risk, demonstrating that he had learned his lesson from the recent Monaco past. After all, the well-known racing motto — 'in order to finish first, you first have to finish' — also applies to second place. As it turned out, he was demoted to fourth in the final standings because of a five-second penalty.

The history of Monaco shows us that desperate actions can lead to serious accidents. Sir Jackie Stewart calls this the result of 'wild speed', when a driver

After Max's first Monaco Grand Prix ended in a heart-stopping crash with Romain Grosjean, it began to seem that the circuit might be jinxed for him.

Yellow flags fly after Max's practice crash at Monaco in 2018
— this was a defining moment.

cannot contain his enthusiasm. He saw this with the young Verstappen during his first encounters with the street circuit.

'As a young and inexperienced driver, you can be very impressed by the stature of Monaco and that can lead to risky emotions,' says Stewart. 'And you must exclude emotions in motor racing. At Monaco, I won my first major international race in Formula 3 and I owed that to my previous career that preceded my time in motor racing. That's where I learned to exclude emotions completely and to approach a race in an extremely calculated way.'

The three-times World Champion didn't reach Formula 1 until he was 25. Prior to that, he had been very successful from an early age in the sport of clay pigeon shooting. By the age of 13 he had already won many awards and become a member of the Scottish national team. He won many national and international competitions and narrowly missed qualifying for the 1960 Olympic Games.

'Shooting taught me the importance of mind management in top sport. I was lucky that I was very successful at it, so I knew the importance of mental strength. One of the lessons I learned was that you shouldn't do things you may regret later. Translating this to Formula 1 means that it isn't the first corner that wins the race, it's the last one.'

Max has learned to love Monaco, but he learned some hard lessons along the way. Perhaps even harder than those he had received from his father. One of very few shaming moments in his entire motorsport career occurred at the street circuit in 2018.

Nothing untoward was going on. The free practice sessions were proceeding smoothly. His Red Bull RB14 was doing what it was supposed to do and so was its driver — until the last lap of free practice. It brought to mind the wise words of Jackie Stewart.

'Don't do anything you might regret later.'

Verstappen did regret it — but learned quickly. Next to father Jos's silent treatment, the 2018 Monaco Grand Prix brought perhaps the most instructive moment of his career.

On the last lap of free practice, prior to qualifying, Verstappen wants to bang out a fast lap. On his way to Rascasse, in the chicane near the swimming pool, things go wrong. Maybe it's Carlos Sainz Jr, who's driving very slowly just before the chicane, or maybe it's over-confidence, causing him to miss the corner and bounce over the kerbs. With all four wheels off the ground, the car is briefly uncontrollable. It hits the guardrail, but not at any great speed. All the same, the car is quite extensively damaged and cannot be repaired before the start of the all-important qualifying battle.

For the first time in his relationship with Helmut Marko, the Red Bull man who originally noticed him, he discovers the Austrian's uncompromising side. When he returns to the pits and encounters his mentor, Marko waves him away in no uncertain terms. All of a sudden, the acclaimed megastar reverts to being the little boy who was reprimanded by his father and put in his place.

Journalist Will Buxton: 'At first Max wanted it all and he wanted it sooner than later. He was furious about not becoming World Champion in his first year. He couldn't be beaten, could he? Then he drove the Red Bull into the crash barriers and his entire weekend was over. For what? What was he going to gain? That was part of Max's immaturity at the time, which he had to work on. He wasn't yet able to see the big picture. Everything was focused on the here and now, precisely because he wanted to achieve everything straight away.'

Like his three previous visits to Monaco, this one was again going to be unremarkable. In those four appearances, the scorecard listed two crashes, a fifth place and a ruined race after the qualifying setback.

After this, however, Max's inherent strength of character immediately re-emerged. When he got to the next Grand Prix, in Canada, without his entourage (father Jos and manager Raymond Vermeulen stay at home), he showed his best side. He finished third, after a calmly executed race weekend. If life is learning, then young Verstappen had learned.

And with that, as Jackie Stewart knows, he took a big step towards the next phase: 'Some drivers are in a racing car or kart from the age of eight and never learn.'

In Max's case, Stewart had the impression that things had worked out well but didn't dare make that claim with any great certainty.

'At the beginning of his career I really wondered if he would be all right. He has improved and I think he has learned. But every now and then the old Max still rears his head. And for someone like me, who doesn't watch a race like a normal spectator, that can be terrifying.'

In that context, we fast-forward to 2021 and the horrific crashes at Silverstone and at the Hungaroring two weeks later.

'That's why I'm not so sure about Max,' observed Stewart after the Silverstone incident. 'Under the same circumstances I would have shifted

Finally he wins in Monaco — celebrations in 2021.

down a gear and taken my chance at another moment. At Silverstone you can also overtake at other places.

'The real greats of Formula 1 don't have big crashes. Stirling Moss had few incidents. Fangio had only one, an almost fatal crash at Monza, but that was caused by exhausting physical effort in the days leading up to the race. Jim Clark died in a Formula 2 race, after a wheel of his Lotus 48 came off. [Nino] Farina and [Alberto] Ascari were in total control. If you go back to the '20s or '30s, drivers didn't have accidents through faults of their own.'

It was great for Max to win at Monaco in 2021. It meant he could shake off that fraught history and also become a local hero — because he lives there too, as a world citizen, near all those other world citizens of Formula 1 who can call themselves Monégasque. Self-respecting Formula 1 drivers live in the principality, where they can move freely among the rich and famous, and where no-one is surprised by a road car like Lewis Hamilton's Pagani Zonda 760 LH with tinted windows, slowly making its way through busy traffic at little more than walking speed.

It's no wonder that the Dutchman has fled to the tax haven. In his own country, he can no longer appear anywhere without encountering hysterical levels of interest.

No matter how casually he deals with fame and fortune, there are limitations. In the Netherlands, he can no longer walk the streets without being accosted. In his own neighbourhood, he may be able to visit his friends in the Pex family, although driving there in an Aston Martin — he owns several of these — would be a striking sight in the Limburg countryside. Usually, though, he simply can't go out in public.

While still on the road to international fame, he and his sponsor from the very beginning wanted to do something special for the Dutch fans, and so the *Jumbo Racedagen* (race days sponsored by the Jumbo supermarket chain) came about at Zandvoort. The event grew into an annual reunion with the Orange Army.

The *Jumbo Racedagen* became a madhouse, especially for him. They were occasions quite unlike anything previously seen in the history of motorsport. No top-level racing, no true spectacle — but hefty entrance charges. For just a few demonstrations with that year's Red Bull. Nothing more than that.

Zandvoort's narrow access roads — only two of them — became completely congested. Just to reach the circuit required hours of queuing,

Max performs for Dutch fans during the 2019 *Jumbo Racedagen* at Zandvoort.

and then, once settled in the dunes or the grandstands, the wait was at least as long. Max's demonstration run in his Red Bull was preceded by a warm-up. Then there was a podium presentation. The Dutch fans were on their feet. For one man and for one car. All right, the supporting programme was quite attractive, but normally no more than a few thousand people would have come to see that.

Even though Max hadn't even turned 20 in 2017, the year of the first of the *Jumbo Racedagen*, he was already carrying the heavy weight of fame on his still narrow shoulders. Everyone wanted something from him. Media people who aren't normally accredited for Formula 1 races saw their chance to ask the new Dutch hero a question: from regional reporters to national sports broadcasters, they lined up to talk to him for a few minutes. Fathers, mothers, children, grandmothers and grandfathers queued up to have a photo taken with him. A lot was allowed.

Max Verstappen made it through those long days at Zandvoort seemingly without effort. It was nevertheless very taxing. All those people. All those questions and all those answers. From early morning until late afternoon. Everyone filmed him. And people ceaselessly waved at him, hoping that he would wave back. He would later admit that these days were considerably harder than a normal race weekend. He had to remain patient, to endure all that interest with a smile, and to do it effortlessly.

Now the *Jumbo Racedagen* belong to the past. Formula 1 has returned to the Netherlands and that relieves Max of the obligation to show up specifically for his fellow countrymen. But those special days showed unequivocally how quickly his star rose. There was no precedent. No other Dutch person could generate so much attention.

In Formula 1, perhaps only Ayrton Senna found comparable fame in his home country. The Brazilian couldn't walk the streets without being besieged by passionate fans. But in Brazil there was no need for fan days, because Brazil had its own Grand Prix. And now so has the Netherlands.

Meanwhile, Monaco is Max Verstappen's new home. In the midst of millionaires and fellow drivers, he can move about freely between all the races and all the obligations.

CHAPTER 14
THE TYRE WHISPERER

L et's go back to that extraordinary victory at the sun-drenched Barcelona circuit, where Max Verstappen became the youngest Grand Prix winner of all time on 15th May 2016. Dutch followers of Formula 1, and certainly his large fanbase, were on the edge of their seats right up to the last lap. Chased by Kimi Räikkönen, he had to go to the limit to keep the Finn's Ferrari behind him.

The Dutch teenager ultimately owed his victory to his tyre management, which allowed him to squeeze out a higher exit speed from the very last corner at Catalunya.

What made that Barcelona finale so intensely exciting? When Max was asked by the Guinness Book of Records how he experienced the final laps of that Spanish Grand Prix, he offered a glimpse into the secrets of the cockpit, into the soul of the athlete on a lonely quest for victory. It's like the tennis player who is leading 40–0 in the deciding set and has three match points, or the cyclist who has built up a lead of minutes on mountain stages and whose victory is almost inevitable, or the football team that's 3–1 up with five minutes to go.

In those final laps, only one thought was running through his head: *make no mistakes, make no mistakes, make no mistakes…. make sure to be first out of the last corner.* The tension was also palpable outside the cockpit. Because even the experts couldn't believe their eyes. The young Dutchman defied the laws of Barcelona, a circuit that's known for devouring tyres. Because of that, everyone wondered when Verstappen would come in for his final tyre change.

We remained in the dark on that score for a long time. Until the last lap. He drove flawlessly, saving his rubber with enough care to cross the finishing line unscathed.

The trickiness of the relationship between track surface and rubber at this particular circuit had been demonstrated three years earlier. In the 2013 Spanish Grand Prix, 82 pitstops were required for 22 cars. More than half the cars made four stops. The chaos surrounding tyre changes and pitstops became so confusing that even the drivers themselves didn't know their positions. Scottish driver Paul di Resta, racing for Force India, lost track and asked his team over the radio: 'Can someone please tell me what's going on?'

The winner of that race, Fernando Alonso, then driving for Ferrari, felt sorry for the spectators.

'I don't have the impression that the people in the stands understood much,' said the Spaniard after his historic home victory. 'It was just a parade and it wasn't about anything.'

Compared with that race, things remained fairly orderly in 2016, with the number of pitstops totalling a mere 48. That a relatively inexperienced young driver could race to victory with only two pitstops seemed unthinkable.

No wonder a lot of people started calling Verstappen 'the tyre whisperer', a term that had surfaced in 2013 in relation to Mexican driver Sergio Pérez. According to tyre specialist Kees van de Grint, there have been many drivers in the past who also knew how to conserve rubber.

'It's a question of temperament,' he says. 'If you're too wild, you'll pay the price. Most drivers have a good grasp of tyre management because there's no other way. If you don't treat the tyres right, you're going to get into trouble. But actually it's more a question of logical thinking than temperament.'

With Max in Spain, and also later in the season at the difficult Suzuka circuit in Japan, Red Bull's entire package was at its best.

'It also has to do with the design of the car,' adds van de Grint. 'Red Bull got it right. Take the steering angle, for example. Most people don't think about that, but steering angle also determines the temperature of the tyres in the corners. If it's too wide, the temperature rises and the tyres become vulnerable. How is the downward pressure and does the suspension function properly? All these technical elements play a role, as does the human factor.

'When the two Mercedes cars crashed out on the first lap of Barcelona, I had a premonition that Max would win.'

Knowledge of tyres and how they function under changing conditions is a crucial component of Formula 1 success. Relatively small contact patches of rubber have to convert the enormous power of today's cars — around 1,000 horsepower — into pure speed.

'Power is worth nothing without good rubber,' says van de Grint. 'The tyres are the most important part of a Formula 1 car. You can have a really powerful engine, but if that power doesn't get to the track, it doesn't help you. Brakes? You can fit the biggest and best, but if the rubber can't take the enormous forces, they won't survive a lap.'

Max Verstappen's tyre management that day in Spain stood out among the 22 drivers, all of whom came from karting. Paul Hembery, Pirelli's motorsport chief at the time, commented afterwards that some drivers can stretch the life of a tyre enough to make a big difference. He thought it was remarkable that Max managed to keep his third set of tyres, mediums, competitive for 32 laps of the 66-lap race at Catalunya.

'Jos and Max were always very alert to the tyre pressure on their karts,' notes van de Grint. 'There's no tyre as critical as a kart tyre. They've taken this knowledge with them to Formula 1.'

Another 2016 race particularly stood out. At the end of the Japanese Grand Prix at Suzuka, Max Verstappen managed to fend off World Champion Lewis Hamilton's attack. A heated debate ensued as to whether the Dutchman's driving had been acceptable.

Defensive driving was a novelty for Verstappen in 2016. In the Toro Rosso, he had been an attacker. In the Red Bull, he also showed that he could excel in defensive tactics.

Perhaps prompted by historical awareness and growing recognition for his immense talent, his defensive driving came to be seen almost as art, as a style of racing that just adds to the spectacle. His duels with Kimi Räikkönen, Sebastian Vettel, Lewis Hamilton and Nico Rosberg were among the finest of that racing year. The aggressor versus the defender — with the defender sitting in his cockpit with the proverbial knife between his teeth.

The showdown at the end of the 1979 French Grand Prix between René Arnoux in his Renault and Gilles Villeneuve in his Ferrari is part of Formula 1 legend. For many laps, the two battled on the very edge, taking enormous risks in their immensely powerful turbocharged cars. Neither gave the other an inch. Racing side by side, braking as late as possible. It was breathtaking.

Duels like this are rare in Formula 1 today. That's why Formula 1 elder Flavio Briatore, who won world titles at Benetton with Michael Schumacher and at Renault with Fernando Alonso, sees Verstappen as such an asset to his sport.

'He drives very aggressively but it's good to see him drive defensively well,' says Briatore. 'That's what people come to see, that's what the public want to see. He's a type of driver that Formula 1 needs. Sport is emotion and you can see that in Max.'

Kees van de Grint thinks that today's complicated rules in Formula 1 don't favour the real racers. When looking back on Verstappen's first season as a Red Bull driver, he judged: 'The FIA welcomes this young guy, the greatest talent to enter the sport this century, so let him race! This boy is magnificent. In karting it's common to race wheel to wheel. Twenty minutes on end, with millimetres between. If there are people who think Max should have let Hamilton pass in Japan, or that he should have opened the door for Räikkönen in Spain, they don't know anything about racing.'

Good management of rubber is the key to success. Although it now seems that a race cannot be completed on a single set of tyres, because the rubber is insufficiently durable and the engines are too powerful, this was possible in 2005, when Fernando Alonso became World Champion. That year, when tyre manufacturers Michelin and Bridgestone were in competition in Formula 1, the regulations were changed to forbid tyre changes during a race, as part of a wider trend of trying to reduce cost. A driver actually had to make do with one set of tyres, even though the cars were pretty much as fast as those of today. Pitstops were only allowed if a tyre suffered damage or if rain fell.

This experiment took an alarming twist in the United States Grand Prix at the Indianapolis Motor Speedway. It was one of the lowest points in the history of Formula 1. The circuit used part of the famous banked oval, notably the high-speed Turn 13 leading onto the start/finish straight. Michelin's rubber couldn't cope. Ralf Schumacher had a huge crash in his Toyota when the left-rear tyre failed in Turn 13, sending the car into the wall. After that, Michelin stated that it couldn't guarantee the safety of the tyres brought to the circuit and withdrew, so only cars with Bridgestones started the race. Six of them. The American crowd was outraged and felt betrayed.

Afterwards, the FIA abandoned its new restriction on tyre changes and then Michelin pulled out. By 2007, only Bridgestone was supplying tyres

Max makes a pitstop for new tyres — this is the Chinese Grand Prix of 2017.

in Formula 1, almost as a gesture of goodwill, because there was now no alternative following Michelin's withdrawal. For 2011, Pirelli won the right to be the single supplier of tyres to all teams through a tender procedure with the FIA.

But still tyre controversies have occurred. Tyres are everything in Formula 1. Because unreliable rubber leads to great danger.

This was demonstrated again in 2013, when tyre hell broke loose in the British Grand Prix at Silverstone. In the race, the left-rear tyres of Lewis Hamilton, Felipe Massa, Jean-Eric Vergne and Sergio Pérez exploded. It was a miracle there were no casualties.

There are other more recent examples. In 2016, Sebastian Vettel's right-rear tyre exploded in Austria, probably because he carried on too long on worn rubber. In 2021, Max Verstappen and Lance Stroll's tyres exploded in Baku, while the cars were close to top speed.

Tyre explosions are always dangerous for the driver, because they happen at high speeds, generally well over 120mph. Yet a racer always wants to race. Even amidst the Michelin tyre debacle at Indianapolis, David Coulthard, for example, just wanted to get out there and drive, even though Michelin had stated that it couldn't guarantee anyone's safety for more than 10 laps.

Sometimes it seems as if a tyre manufacturer can never get it right. Kees van de Grint knows all about that. He was, he says, a 'Formula 1 Kwik-Fit' in his last year with Bridgestone: 'With the teams at the front you did well and you were welcome to come for a drink. But the drivers at the back always blamed the tyres. Meanwhile they conveniently forgot that the chassis and the driver also determine the behaviour of the tyre.'

A Formula 1 tyre is a technological *tour de force*. The tyres have to absorb forces up to 6G for an hour and a half, under varying conditions from hot to cold, on different surfaces. The wear and tear are enormous, as can be seen from the 'marbles' — balls of rubber deposited as tyres become worn — that become littered across a track as a race progresses.

For a 'newbie' Formula 1 fan, perhaps attracted by the success of Max Verstappen, a race without expert commentary is difficult to follow. The tyre regulations may be understandable to anyone who has been watching the sport for years, but sometimes even for them it can be difficult to grasp.

Pirelli continues to be Formula 1's sole supplier and determines the tyre package for a race weekend. Nowadays the company offers five compounds of dry tyre for use over the course of a season and labels them C1, C2, C3, C4

The 2016 Austrian Grand Prix provided a good example of Max looking after his tyres: he completed all but 16 laps of the race on one set.

and C5, with C1 being the hardest and C5 the softest. For each race weekend, Pirelli nominates three of these compounds and identifies them for teams and fans by colours on the sidewalls: white is the hardest, which lasts the longest; yellow signifies the medium compound; and red is the softest, which of course is the fastest but also wears out quickly. Two other colours, green and blue, are used for wet conditions.

At the 2016 Austrian Grand Prix, Verstappen surprised friend and foe by completing no fewer than 56 laps of the race on 'soft' tyres after doing the first 16 laps on 'supersofts' (using the tyre nomenclature of the time). With this he confirmed his reputation as a 'tyre whisperer'. But was it hubris? Was it lack of experience?

Then a few months later, after the United States Grand Prix, he suddenly received criticism from an unexpected direction. His mentor, Helmut Marko, pointed out to the media and the public that his protégé still had some way to go, stating in no uncertain terms that Verstappen's tyre wear had been too high in that race.

The criticism really was a surprise. After all, fans and journalists had already hoisted Max up as a paragon of tyre management. But he was human as well. In his unbridled ambition, he raced too hard. After the team told him to slow down to conserve his tyres, he parried through the microphone: 'I didn't come here to finish fourth.' That remark didn't go down well. 'If you can't pass them,' Marko told a reporter from *Auto Motor und Sport*, 'you can't overuse the tyres. Then you don't win races and certainly not championships.' Marko also compared Verstappen to Ricciardo: 'Compared to Daniel, Max had higher tyre wear.'

For a moment the myth was shattered. It must have been a lesson in humility. This was the race in which Max also made an unannounced pitstop, and thus misled the team, and in which he later crashed out. It was a painful moment of inexperience on the long road to the future.

CHAPTER 15
HELMUT MARKO

Mercedes had Niki Lauda, whose blunt and authentic views about Formula 1 were a breath of fresh air across the paddock. Similarly, journalists have always liked to listen to Sir Jackie Stewart, because people who have made history in Formula 1, in his case as a driver and a team owner, usually tell it straight. Formula 1 veterans like Lauda (who died in 2019) and Stewart (who makes few media appearances these days) are often missed, if only because of their independent nature.

But then we do still have Helmut Marko. He's of that old school. The Austrian is generally regarded as the man who discovered Max. He's an ex-racer of whom Gijs van Lennep, his team-mate when they won the Le Mans 24 Hours together, says 'fuel, rather than blood, flows through his veins'.

Marko's tirade against Max Verstappen after the young driver's blunder in the final free practice sessions at Monaco in 2018 showed an important element of his character. Emotional, still in his old age, and critical without worrying about personal feelings. His furious gestures after Max's pointless accident, one that had major consequences for the team, revealed all: Marko isn't a man for bullshit or excuses. Or, as Will Buxton says, 'He's very straightforward and that reveals itself in such moments.'

The Austrian is a striking figure in the Formula 1 paddock. Aged nearly 80, he commands respect from young and old. Most of the time he comes across as a friendly old fellow, as on the Dutch television talk show *Jinek*, in which he explained to the audience, speaking gently and warmly, how he put

Max into Formula 1 and how father Jos reacted, bewildered and speechless, when he told him on the phone.

Marko's own racing career ended in 1972 after an incident in the French Grand Prix at Clermont-Ferrand when driving for BRM. A stone thrown up by the car in front penetrated his visor and went into his left eye. He remembers it vividly: 'The pain was immense... but I managed to stay conscious. I managed to pull the car over and then I lost consciousness.' Subsequently, visor specifications were upgraded and other drivers have benefited from his misfortune.

He has had a glass eye ever since. It's the same grey-green as his good eye and the eyelid blinks as if nothing is wrong. The handicap only becomes visible when his right eye moves and the left one doesn't.

Behind Marko's charming demeanour, passion manifests itself frequently in emotional outbursts — highs and lows — about the Red Bull team's performance. He's just about the most quoted man in the paddock. Christian Horner may be the boss of Red Bull, but Helmut Marko, the right-hand man, seems to be the team's conscience. With every controversy, large or small, his name pops up. On social media, Formula 1 websites, mainstream media. As journalist David Tremayne says, 'I sometimes wonder where he gets the energy from. Not so long ago I was writing five books in a year. Now I'm a bit older I wonder how on earth I managed to do that.'

Marko is always there, everywhere. He's the guardian who watches over Red Bull's drivers, the shrewd talent scout who can read a young driver's character like an open book.

When he first chats with a promising young driver, it normally takes about 20 minutes. His first interview with the teenage Max Verstappen lasted an hour and a half.

'When he was still only 15, I had a long talk with him, but it was as if I was talking to a 25-year-old who had just left university. Apart from his racing talent, he has so many other interests. He knows what's going on in the world. For us, that was the reason to put him in a Formula 1 car. Because I was convinced that he could do it.'

'Was it not a big risk, were there no doubts at all?' the interviewer on *Jinek* asked.

Marko smiled modestly. With a mischievous twinkle in his eye, he answered: 'No risk, no fun.'

That's the true Helmut Marko. He's one of the driving forces behind

Red Bull's Helmut Marko listens to his protégé at the
Hungarian Grand Prix of 2019.

the success of the Red Bull Formula 1 team. Outspoken, confrontational, straightforward, sometimes controversial, generally impeccable. His opinions sometimes shake the sport to its foundations. He's critical of anyone and everyone who, in his view, makes a mess of things. He became a thorn in the side of Toto Wolff, boss of Mercedes. It happened as well with engine supplier Renault.

He also discovered Sebastian Vettel, with whom Red Bull won four world titles in a row (from 2010 to 2013) before Mercedes steamrollered its way to Formula 1 supremacy.

Marko snatched Verstappen from the clutches of rivals. The boy was racing in Formula 3 and his reputation already preceded him. Marko struck before other lurking bidders managed to catch him. Mercedes, for one, wanted to offer Verstappen a contract, albeit not directly for a Formula 1 seat. There were other options too: Max was already on the radar for a place in the junior programmes at Ferrari, which had already been impressed by his qualities in Florida, and at McLaren.

Marko's decisive action led to a match made in heaven. Max Verstappen and Red Bull became a combination as strong as Lewis Hamilton and Mercedes. Unshakeable, with a loyalty that borders on love. As in every marriage, though, there have been moments when the partners started doubting each other. It happened when Max was too wild and impatient, when his aggressive driving style went over the edge. It happened when Red Bull just couldn't put together the winning combination of chassis and engine during those years with Renault. Things often went wrong between the team and its engine supplier, so much so that there were moments when both parties had to bite their tongues to avoid saying something they would later regret.

'They were lost years,' says Peter Windsor of the period with Renault engines up to the end of 2018. 'These years slowed things down. I remember very well that I found Helmut in the paddock and started chatting to him. I thought they should have gone with Honda. But he was irritated, as if it was the stupidest suggestion anyone had ever made. Two years later they went with Honda.

'Max could have won Grands Prix two years earlier. There was absolutely no chemistry between Red Bull and Renault.'

Could that have had anything to do with old English/French grudges in the middle of Brexit? Or something from the past? French nonchalance doesn't align with Austrian pragmatism. During his interview with *Jinek*, Marko said that after his accident in France in 1972, the emergency services were hopeless. Two nearby hospitals were closed that Sunday and, at a third one, a surgeon had to be dragged away from a family barbecue to operate on the injured eye.

The collaboration with Renault was compromised from the start. Red Bull wanted the engine division to be in Milton Keynes, to allow the collaboration to be as close as possible. With the difficulties intensifying in later years, this compromised relationship may well have cost Max Verstappen the one record that he, and Helmut Marko, wanted so badly — the achievement of youngest ever Formula 1 World Champion. That honour remains with Sebastian Vettel, Marko's former protégé, probably forever. Not that Verstappen or Marko let statistics become too important — but, still, that one would have been a nice one.

'It was a missed opportunity,' says Windsor of Red Bull's tardiness in going with Honda. 'I was sure McLaren had no idea how to get a good deal with those Honda people, but Adrian Newey did. He would have been able to get Honda to Milton Keynes, as it is now.'

McLaren had a disastrous year in 2015 with the Honda engines supplied from Japan. The hopelessness was illustrated by that moment in Brazil when Fernando Alonso, after the car had failed yet again, this time during qualifying, relaxed in a deckchair and sunbathed. He knew, of course, that this image would circulate around the world and be seen as a statement about his failing team.

The sensitivity of the relationship between engine manufacturer and racing team has seldom been as clear as it was in that instance. Just as the relationship between McLaren and Honda was doomed to fail, Red Bull and Renault were mismatched. Now each of these top teams has a new partner and both have risen Phoenix-like from the ashes.

Gijs van Lennep won the 1971 Le Mans 24 Hours with Helmut Marko, driving the fabled Porsche 917. When asked to unearth some of his ex-partner's qualities, the Dutchman has to dig deep into his memory.

'He was just like me... a fast, intelligent driver. He shifted very accurately and kept the gearbox in such good condition that we were able to sell it as new after the race. Other drivers broke the gearboxes. We didn't. That's how we were able to win, by keeping the car in one piece.

'I also raced with him in the Alfa Romeo team on the Targa Florio in

1972,' adds van Lennep. 'He was unbelievably fast.' In that arduous Sicilian race, held on a 45-mile course through mountains, Marko finished a fighting second, lapping a whole two minutes a lap quicker than anyone else at the end.

That Le Mans victory was really the only major racing success Marko ever achieved. A couple of months later he made his Formula 1 début in his home race, in Austria at the circuit now known as the Red Bull Ring, coincidentally when compatriot Niki Lauda also raced a Formula 1 car for the first time. But less than a year later Marko's unfortunate accident in the French Grand Prix brought an early and abrupt end to his driving career.

The traumatic experience of losing an eye, he said in an interview for the official Formula 1 website, has had a major impact on his life. 'Just get this: an injury in the eye is very painful. They had to sew the eye, so every blink was a horror. I couldn't sleep for many nights also because I still was full of the idea that motor racing is the only reason to live.'

That explains almost everything.

'If you're like me,' continues van Lennep, 'you've got the racing bug and then you just can't imagine a life without motor racing.'

Marko grew up with Jochen Rindt, who posthumously became Formula 1 World Champion in 1970, and together they became enthralled by motor racing. In the same interview Marko talked about that background.

'The first race we visited was Nürburgring in 1961. We both had failed our university entrance diploma and instead of going home and telling the sobering news decided to go to a race. We drove all night to Nürburgring. We parked in the woods and slept in the car and woke up the next morning from the noise of the Formula 1 cars. Jochen immediately said: "That's for me, that is what I want to do!" We were sitting devotedly in the grass listening to the sound of the cars and after a few laps were able to say whether it was a Ferrari passing or a Matra or a Cosworth-powered car. I was 18 and Jochen was 19.'

After Rindt reached Formula 1, Marko also saw opportunities for himself in racing but only got going after graduating as a lawyer in 1967. He never practised in that profession, however, because motorsport took over. His active career, starting in Formula Vee single-seaters at the same time as Lauda, lasted only four and a half seasons. Even after his accident, returning to a career in law wasn't on his agenda and he stayed in motor racing. He couldn't live without it.

Gijs van Lennep: 'He's no longer in it for the money. He's addicted to racing. It keeps him going and it seems to keep him on his toes.'

In Austria in 2014, Helmut Marko was reunited with a 1972 BRM, joined by
Red Bull's then World Champion Sebastian Vettel (left) and fellow Austrian
Formula 1 veterans Niki Lauda (centre) and Gerhard Berger.

Will Buxton: 'Helmut is similar to Bernie Ecclestone. These are people who have racing and motorsport so mixed in with their blood that they can't live without it.'

Max Verstappen was 15 when Marko first noticed him. That's three years younger than Marko was himself when he was in those German woods musing about Formula 1 with Rindt. Sixty years later, he's still hanging out with drivers who could be his grandsons. But age is irrelevant when people share a passion.

'His great strength is his clarity,' says van Lennep. 'In a sport with so many variables, that's a quality that appeals to a younger driver. That's why he gets on so well with Max Verstappen and before that with Sebastian Vettel and Daniel Ricciardo.'

That clarity is best conveyed with some of Marko's own words. Here are some quotes:

On danger: 'In Formula 1 there has to be a certain amount of risk. If you're afraid of that, you should become a taxi driver.'

On the past: 'Times have changed so much that stories about the cars I drove are just a waste of time.'

On the money today's drivers earn: 'You get paid 100 times more than we did back then... you have a lot less work in much safer cars. So enjoy it and be grateful.'

On his wealth of experience: 'That's simply the balance of 50 active years in motorsport. With so much experience you can say to a driver, for example in Monaco: try a different line; approach a race weekend as efficiently as possible; don't try to be the fastest on Friday, save something for qualifying.'

Marko's lessons, as those around him know, are unequivocal. In a way, for Max, he has taken over Jos's role.

Will Buxton: 'Helmut always says, "Do as you've been taught and everything will be fine." He doesn't teach you how to race. If you enter Formula 1 and get a contract, you can already race very well. His approach is completely bizarre: he can utterly destroy someone or put them on a pedestal. I've heard stories of him and Jochen borrowing his father's cars and driving them without permission. If they crashed or got into trouble, they were on their own.

'That's how he is. If you put yourself in a position, you're responsible for your performance. If you can't handle that pressure, that's your problem, not his. Yes, that's very harsh. Some drivers benefit from it, others go completely off the rails. It's interesting that some drivers felt the Sword of Damocles hanging over their heads. That has never been the case with Max, because he has never let the team down and therefore has never felt threatened. Max was never told to perform better, otherwise he could leave.

'Helmut has a thing for Max, just as he had a thing for Seb Vettel. At Red Bull they were shocked when Vettel left for Ferrari. Helmut sees a young Seb in Max, someone who will remain loyal and never abandon ship. They never expected Seb to leave and yet he went. That did hurt. But with Max, Helmut has discovered a new relationship with a loyal and strong driver.'

How this happened is told in the documentary *Whatever It Takes*, which was made under the auspices of the Verstappens themselves. It was Marko's determination that brought Max under Red Bull's wing with a seat at Toro Rosso. After the Verstappens visited Red Bull at the German Grand Prix in 2014 and the cards were on the table, Niki Lauda phoned to ask if they would also like to come and see Mercedes. Soon after, Marko contacted Jos and made the offer that Verstappen senior accepted: two years with Toro Rosso… immediately.

Marko knew what he was getting into. By bringing Max to the team, he got something extra — the Verstappen family itself. With all his accumulated wisdom, Marko could handle that very well.

'We at Red Bull love characters. They're allowed to have an opinion and that's fine.'

Moving forward to May 2016, Marko had another important meeting with the Verstappens. After the Russian Grand Prix, he invited them to lunch with him in Graz, Austria, and told them that Max was going to be promoted from Toro Rosso to Red Bull after one season and four races. Max's first race for Red Bull, the Spanish Grand Prix, proved Marko right, so much so that the victory tasted like sweet revenge on all the critics who hadn't liked the idea of a young boy joining a top team. As Marko put it, 'There were so many negative comments about what we were doing.'

After years of struggle and uncertainty, victory in that Spanish Grand Prix for Max Verstappen — and through him for Helmut Marko — came as a gift from heaven, handed to them by a Mercedes mess-up. It was one of the highlights of Marko's 50-year career.

'If I had to name three,' he has said several times in interviews, 'they would be my victory at Le Mans, Sebastian Vettel's first world title at Red Bull and Max's victory in Barcelona. Because let's face it: that's the stuff dreams are made of, isn't it?'

CHAPTER 16
SIR JACKIE STEWART

Helmut Marko says that discussing Formula 1's great drivers of the past is a waste of time because the differences between their cars and those of today are so great that any comparison is meaningless. Perhaps they don't always bring agreeable memories either, the cars of the past. Loved by purists, yes, but feared by protagonists.

Sir Jackie Stewart was a three-times World Champion (1969, 1971 and 1973) in cars that would be deemed suicidal today. No sensible person would want to get into one of his Matras or Tyrrells nowadays and race it in anger. In Stewart's day, drivers dropped like flies, like soldiers in the trenches. During his active racing years, he saw 57 drivers perish, including many illustrious friends and colleagues. They included Bruce McLaren, Jochen Rindt, Pedro Rodríguez, Jo Siffert and François Cevert. The last of these, Cevert, was Stewart's Tyrrell protégé and team-mate. The Frenchman was killed during qualifying for the 1973 United States Grand Prix, a race that was to have been Stewart's farewell before retiring — but he pulled out.

Stewart was a relentless promoter of safety during his era, a time when circuit owners and team bosses took little notice of it. The racetracks were arenas of death, Roman colosseums of the 20th century. One was Zandvoort, where the Dutch Grand Prix was twice blighted in the space of only three years, with the fatal crashes of Piers Courage (1970) and Roger Williamson (1973). Between those tragedies, the undulating track amidst sand dunes had received so much criticism, led by Stewart, that the Dutch Grand Prix of 1972 was cancelled because the drivers refused to race there.

Through Stewart's leadership, the Grand Prix Drivers' Association of the time acted, in effect, as a safety committee that reviewed circuits and made recommendations for improvements. He didn't make many friends with this campaign, but his dogged efforts in the face of sustained opposition ultimately led to international motorsport becoming very much less dangerous. But never risk-free.

Nowadays, Stewart sees new dangers looming in Formula 1, with more fearless driving, more heated rivalries, and more invulnerability felt by drivers in their super-strong carbon-fibre cocoons. Some severe crashes of recent years — Romain Grosjean's narrow escape from a burning Haas car in Bahrain in 2020 or the tyre blow-outs experienced by Max Verstappen and Lance Stroll in Azerbaijan in 2021 — could have gone awfully wrong. And then there were the serious clashes of 2021 between Max Verstappen and Lewis Hamilton. First came Silverstone, where the Dutchman thumped the barrier with incredible force. Then there was Monza, where the Red Bull climbed over the Mercedes, one of its rear wheels hitting the silver car's halo. These violent accidents could have ended very differently.

Is it a coincidence that Max Verstappen has been involved rather too often? That's what Sir Jackie wonders. The incidents of 2021 have led to new discussions about safety in which Stewart is regularly quoted. He agreed to be interviewed for this book after the Silverstone crash but before the Monza one.

The Scottish sage has developed a subdued respect for the young Dutchman. As a distinguished former racer, he sees Max's enormous potential and loves his character, but doesn't close his eyes to what he sees as darker sides of an extraordinary talent. Hardcore Verstappen fans, as well as Red Bull's team management, haven't been happy with Stewart's opinions and — understandably — don't agree with them.

In his autobiography *Winning Is Not Enough*, Stewart made a powerful observation: 'From my youth... I have believed that real, lasting success is defined not only by the accumulation of winning but also by the manner of victory. It's not enough simply to win. It is considerably more profound if success is achieved with integrity and care.'

Stewart converted that into a formula: 'Winning (over a long period of time) + Integrity + Care = Success'.

This concept may seem dated. After all, winning every corner is what

While Red Bull Team Principal Christian Horner looks on,
Sir Jackie Stewart chats with Max, in Canada in 2016.

today's generation of drivers, including Max Verstappen, are all about. As drivers have become virtually invulnerable, the limit of mortal danger has been stretched. In his period, Stewart says, drivers were more prepared for the unexpected.

Another favoured Stewart word is 'grace'. If you want to stay at the top, he believes, there's more to it than just winning. In the longer term, world titles achieved with grace are more valuable and have more importance. Formula 1 history has shown that all kinds of drivers have become World Champions and heroes of their chosen sport, but only a few have risen higher still.

Will Max ever get there?

'He certainly isn't a legend yet, but he can become one. Max is still in the learning phase. A lot of these guys have been in a race car or kart since they were eight years old, but some of them will never learn. That in turn has to do with mental attitude, which only the absolute top athletes have.'

Even Lewis Hamilton hasn't always been able to resist the enormous pressure. Even he, the most successful Formula 1 driver of all time, holder of the most pole positions and victories, isn't immune to mental lapses, as during 2021 at the restart in Azerbaijan and when he hit the pitlane wall in Russia — both rookie mistakes.

Mental calmness, says Stewart, is an essential trait for a successful and honourable winner.

Stewart's fundamentals were shaped by clay pigeon shooting, which requires a mindset of ultimate focus. He says that mental equilibrium is always necessary in motor racing.

'Mind management in a race car isn't any more difficult than when shooting, I have learned. If you're somewhat unsettled by tension, the first shot becomes more difficult, which also applies to the start of a race. The difference is that in a race you still have time to compensate for a mistake, but with a wrong shot you don't.'

Thoughtfulness is also part of Stewart's curriculum for the successful Formula 1 driver. From the past, greats like Argentine Juan Manuel Fangio and Frenchman Alain Prost were among the most thoughtful of drivers. Prost, whom Stewart observed racing at first-hand, demonstrated mastery in every fibre of his being, which earned him the nickname 'The Professor'. Prost exemplified mind management *par excellence*.

The character of a driver is reflected in his driving style. Stewart mentions the differences between Prost and Senna, who fought legendary duels in their period, as Verstappen and Hamilton do now.

'Senna was exciting, but as a driver I preferred Prost. If you look back at some races, for example Monaco, where a lot of steering movements are necessary, you see that Senna was much more nervous. Prost drove more fluently. Senna was marginally influenced by emotions, Prost was not.

'With Max, I see him sometimes getting angry, or sounding irritated over the radio. I have learned in my time always to control my emotions. Emotions in this sport are dangerous.'

In Stewart's period, of course, there was no on-board radio. In today's Formula 1 it's part of the show, recording every breath and — depending on the entertainment value and language used — passing it on, filtered, to the eager audience.

Max's on-board radio demeanour is the mirror of his soul, even though the public doesn't hear everything. Even after the races, his unmistakable body language and sharp statements underline this, as in the confrontation with Esteban Ocon in Brazil in 2018, after the backmarker had punted him out of the lead. In many aspects of his character, the Verstappen DNA is plain to see. But that's exactly what Red Bull values so much in him. It's what the Orange Army likes, too, and why his competitors and team-mates respect him.

Stewart has a more nuanced view. He doesn't like to watch the 'wild driving' that occasionally defined Verstappen in the early years. It reminds him too much of the dark days of Formula 1. As he sees it, the sport is becoming increasingly dangerous due to recklessness and excessively intense rivalry.

'Silverstone 2021 could have ended in tears,' he says again, 'and Formula 1 almost lost a promising new star.'

Perhaps Stewart is a voice in the wilderness. After all, when the express train of Formula 1 seasons rush past, there's almost no time to look back. The show must go on, as it always has. And why not? The alarming accidents of recent years have increased the entertainment value without the grim consequences of actual casualties.

This makes it harder for Stewart to watch the races nowadays. It's as if death is being challenged, laughed at almost, and he has lived through too much tragedy to take it lightly.

'There are two problems in racing today. The first is that the penalties are far too light. That 10-second penalty for Lewis at Silverstone was a joke. Secondly, the drivers think they're invulnerable. They don't know the seriousness of the danger anymore. In every race nowadays they make contact, causing damage to the front wings. In my day that was unthinkable, because you were playing with death.'

The only fatality in the modern era of Formula 1 was that of Jules Bianchi, who crashed in Japan in 2014, before the introduction of halo cockpit protection, and died nine months later. It wasn't a real racing accident, as the Frenchman slid helplessly under a crane that was lifting another car over the fence on the soaking wet Suzuka track. Since then, circuit safety in general has been further improved and the rules concerning use of safety cars and yellow flags have been tightened.

Circuit safety, as we have seen, was a major concern for Stewart in his day. Another target of his campaigning was the *Nordschleife* at the Nürburgring — which he nicknamed 'The Green Hell'. Even though he had famously conquered the infamous 14-mile circuit himself in the most atrocious weather, winning the 1968 German Grand Prix by over four minutes, he wasn't thanked for leading a boycott of the track in 1970. For that, he even received death threats from Germany, way before the age of social media.

At the time, drivers weren't important voices in the Formula 1 circus. In the eyes of promoters and team owners, their job was to perform, not to criticise. After all, they were replaceable, even if they were World Champions. But driving at 'The Green Hell' was a step too far, even for the bravest of the brave.

'If it's so dangerous, why are we going to drive there?' Stewart asked his colleagues.

'Because if we don't, we will be accused of being cowards,' some of them replied.

Jochen Rindt, who himself perished at Monza in 1970, felt provoked by that attitude and said: 'I'm not afraid of anything, but if my car, for example due to a technical defect, goes off the track at 150mph, I would rather not hit a tree.'

Racing drivers will always push the limits. It's the very definition of what they do. And Formula 1 audiences love that. In fact, a spectacular crash is a good antidote to declining viewer ratings.

Max Verstappen's gritty combativeness may have become compelling for today's audiences, but Stewart hopes the Dutchman will remain in control of his character.

'In Formula 1 you have to grow up sooner rather than later. I think he can

'Verstappen is taking longer than expected to mature.' That was the view
expressed by Sir Jackie Stewart after this collision with
Lewis Hamilton in the 2021 Italian Grand Prix.

be a frequent World Champion, a top-class racer, but he would go even faster if he was a bit less aggressive.'

After the clash between Hamilton and Verstappen in Italy in 2021, the Scot dropped all of his reservations. Speaking to the *Daily Mail*, the British newspaper, he said:

'Verstappen is taking longer than expected to mature. Not even to go to see Hamilton after a serious accident when you have just driven over the top of the guy is something I don't really understand. Especially when he is still in his car and remained there for a long time before getting out.

'Max has quite a lot to learn. But who will he listen to?

'He's very, very good. He's probably the fastest driver on the grid now, but to be a proper champion you cannot be entangling yourself in crashes all the time.'

Stewart's own son, Paul, pursued a racing career but realised he wasn't good enough for Formula 1 and his ambitions concluded in the now-defunct Formula 3000 category. Stewart would have preferred his son not to race but decided to involve himself rather than leave that to others. Nowadays, would he be happy if one of his grandchildren drove in Formula 1?

'I don't know. Ultimately it would be their own choice, but to be honest, I would have my doubts about that. Not just because of the speed or the danger, but also because it's a very complicated world.'

The father/son factor is interesting. There has been a small army of racing fathers with sons who have followed in their footsteps: just in Formula 1 we've had Graham and Damon Hill, Gilles and Jacques Villeneuve, Mario and Michael Andretti, Keke and Nico Rosberg… amongst others. Usually the fathers have set the highest of benchmarks, leaving the sons with a huge challenge to surpass them. Stewart notes that this wasn't the case with the Verstappens.

'Jos is a bit of an exception to the rule where fathers did very well in Formula 1. Although Jos did quite well, still, I only hope that he can still make his influence felt. When you're as successful as Max, have won so many Grands Prix and are so popular, it's hard to change certain behaviours. Jos can still help, as long as Max listens to him.'

Arriving young in Formula 1 is still quite a novelty but in Stewart's time it was almost unheard of. You had to be mature, mentally and physically. He himself didn't reach Formula 1 until the age of 25, after giving up a long and successful career in clay pigeon shooting. He ended up in a racing car more or less by coincidence. His father was a garage owner and one of his customers asked if young Jackie would like to try his Porsche in a competition. Soon the 21-year-old fell under the spell of motor racing, just as his older brother Jimmy had done. Initially Jackie did it secretly, because Jimmy's activities terrified his mother and she didn't want her other son getting involved as well. He registered at his first local races as 'A.N. Other', to prevent his new passion becoming a source of irritation at the dinner table. The rest is history.

Unlike Max, Jackie Stewart had to do it all on his own, helped by what he'd learned in shooting.

'I learned to eliminate emotion. You must never get angry. When I saw Max drive at the beginning of his career, I thought he exaggerated his aggression a bit and wondered if things would work out. Over the years he has learned, but whether it's enough remains to be seen.'

After the big crash at Silverstone in 2021, it all went wrong again a fortnight later in Hungary. This time it was clearly a case of bad luck, with Valtteri Bottas causing a multi-car incident at the first corner that put Verstappen out of contention for the rest of the race. In this sport, which depends on so many factors, with so many variables possible, luck steps in from time to time to play a crucial role.

That's why the 2021 season remained one of blood-curdling excitement until the last lap of the last Grand Prix in Abu Dhabi. Indeed, before these unlucky moments for Verstappen, he had had a comfortable lead over Hamilton. But there's a downside to the definition of luck. If winners take all, it means that losers bring bad luck upon themselves. Was that the case with the tyre blow-out in Baku or the collision in Hungary caused by Bottas?

At the end of the day, however, there's only one inalienable law: 'To finish first, you first have to finish.'

Jackie Stewart wrote about luck in *Winning Is Not Enough*, talking about his 1969 season when he became World Champion for the first time driving a Matra for Ken Tyrrell. Specifically, he had ascribed his victory in that year's Spanish Grand Prix to 'good luck':

> I understood good luck but, as time went by, I didn't really believe in bad luck. In motor racing, as in other areas of life, you often hear people complaining about their bad luck, claiming nothing is going their way. More often than not, a closer inspection suggests their problems are the result of human error, whether it is bad planning,

bad structuring, bad preparation or bad judgement. A racing driver curses his 'ill fortune' when his car suffers a mechanical failure, but luck often has little to do with it. The failure will usually have been caused by poor concept engineering, or a flaw in manufacturing, casting or machining, or maybe the incorrect assembly of a particular component.

A few pages later he returned to the subject when discussing the dramatic finish to that same year's Italian Grand Prix at Monza, where victory confirmed him as World Champion:

Incredibly, after 240 miles of racing, less than a fifth of a second covered the first four cars. In truth, any of us might have claimed the victory but, to my great delight and relief, it was me whose car found something extra to win the race by a hair's breadth from Jochen Rindt, with Jean-Pierre Beltoise third and Bruce McLaren fourth.

What separated the cars in such a blanket finish? Some might say it was luck. Once again, I would take issue with that. In my view, it was no accident that the Matra-Ford crossed the line first. The fact is we had spent a substantial part of the practice and qualifying sessions on the Saturday painstakingly taking time to ensure I had gear ratios that enabled me to accelerate out of the Parabolica, the last corner before the home straight, and then only have to change from third to fourth gear before crossing the line. That exhaustive process involved calculating exactly how much fuel the car would be carrying and the likely weight of the car on that final lap — all to get the gear ratios exactly right. It may have seemed an enormous amount of work to secure a tiny advantage but, from the Parabolica to the finish line, each of the other drivers had to change gears from third to fourth and then to fifth. Every time you change a gear, you risk making a mistake, which could cost you a fraction of a second — and, at that speed, that could equate to as much as 40 or 50 metres. In such a tight finish, that apparently insignificant attention to detail gave me those few extra inches, and that proved the difference between winning and losing because I won the race by a distance of just 12 inches.'

Jos Verstappen drove for the Stewart Formula 1 team in 1998.

It's all so marginal: good luck or bad, winning or losing, hero or zero. One driver becomes a legend, the other dissolves into obscurity like sugar in hot water. Moreover, fate isn't only in the hands of the driver. Success also very much depends on circumstances and the team.

'I hope Max becomes legendary, but there are no guarantees, you have to stay alert. You don't become a legend if you've won a few races. Changes in regulations can throw the whole thing off course. We went from a 1,500cc engine to 3,000cc and that completely changed the pecking order. When I was in the Matra, everyone had the same engine, the Ford Cosworth. And that created a level playing field, which I very much favour. Jochen Rindt was a great friend of mine, but he never got an engine that was better. That was fair. Anyone could buy a Cosworth for £7,000 and race with it. Nobody got the benefit of a few seconds or a bit more horsepower. That was a unique situation, but it could only work because of the integrity of Cosworth. It was fantastic racing, because nobody had the advantage of a more powerful engine. It was just about driving.

'In recent years Mercedes has been supreme, which has allowed Lewis to win. But nobody knows how good the other driver really is when the material is unevenly matched.'

The arrival of Max Verstappen, Stewart believes, has done Formula 1 enormous good. The Orange Army especially impresses the distinguished three-times World Champion.

'Lewis also has many fans, but they're not as passionate as Max's. He's the first big Dutchman in this sport and that's great for Formula 1. In addition, he presents himself very well and does well with the media. And all this before he's even at the peak of his career.'

CHAPTER 17
SECRETS OF THE STEERING WHEEL

Max Verstappen has spent his entire Formula 1 career at teams owned by Austrian billionaire Dietrich Mateschitz, whose estimated wealth in 2021, according to Forbes, was $25.4 billion. All of this has been generated from a brand of energy drink consumed in massive quantities around the world, especially by young people. Red Bull, the drink, has its origins in Thailand, where it was created as *Krating Daeng* (meaning 'Red Bull') by entrepreneur Chaleo Yoovidhya in partnership with Mateschitz in 1984, then licensed elsewhere, starting in Austria in 1987.

In 2004, Mateschitz took over the ailing Jaguar Formula 1 team, which in turn had evolved from the Stewart team run by Jackie and Paul Stewart, and renamed it Red Bull Racing. The brand is synonymous with success. Everything Mateschitz touches turns to gold. In Austria, he's held in high esteem not only because of his Formula 1 presence but also through his ownership of FC Salzburg football club and the A1 Ring, the Austrian circuit originally called the Österreichring and now known as the Red Bull Ring.

Mateschitz introduced to Formula 1 the system of A and B teams, between which drivers can switch seats without any difficult contract negotiations. In football, this concept is as old as the ball itself. Talents start at AlphaTauri, which was known as Toro Rosso until the end of 2019 and came into Mateschitz's ownership as Minardi at the end of 2005. When a young driver has proved his qualities at the 'junior' team, he's allowed to move up to the 'senior' team, Red Bull, with its better, faster cars. Until the introduction of a cost cap in Formula 1 for the 2021 season, Red Bull's budget was more than three times that of AlphaTauri's.

Before Max Verstappen's promotion from Toro Rosso to Red Bull in May 2016, the concept had worked well twice before. In 2009, Sebastian Vettel was elevated to the A team, winning his third race as a Red Bull driver and the following year taking the first of four consecutive World Championship titles. In 2013, Daniel Ricciardo went the same way: he didn't become World Champion but he did win eight Grands Prix during the course of five seasons.

Ricciardo was 27 years old when Verstappen became his team-mate. The sympathetic, good-humoured Australian, who started drinking champagne from his shoe after a victory, suddenly seemed to find a second wind. Verstappen brought new life to the team and pushed Ricciardo, who was now concerned about being outperformed by a teenager, in practice, qualifying and races. This made Red Bull a proper mid-season rival to the dominant Mercedes of Lewis Hamilton and Nico Rosberg. Max won in Spain, Daniel in Malaysia. Ferrari suddenly had nowhere to go and in the battle for the runner-up position in the constructors' title the Austrian team overtook the Italian one.

The Max Factor worked immediately, from the first race, although a whimsical twist of fate was also involved. The victory in Barcelona was partly a fluke, preceded by the two Mercedes drivers taking each other out, but all the same no-one could have guessed that the Dutchman would secure his win so skilfully. Least of all he himself. 'It's a completely new car, I really need to get used to it,' he had said beforehand.

By contrast, Daniil Kvyat, who went the opposite way, from Red Bull to Toro Rosso, struggled with his unfamiliar car that weekend. He said of the differences between them: 'I drove the Red Bull for a year and a half and I got very used to it. This car [the Toro Rosso] is much more direct, much sharper. The balance is very different and I have to adapt my whole driving style, which is not easy for a Formula 1 driver.'

He might just as well have said: 'I've ended up in a shitty car that steers badly, sometimes with too much oversteer, other times with lots of understeer.'

All this implies that Verstappen's performance in the Toro Rosso had been almost supernatural. The teenager showed in 2016 that, like Michael Schumacher upon his arrival at Ferrari, he was capable of taking a team to the next level.

While Kvyat struggled with his new car, Verstappen had virtually no

Dietrich Mateschitz, Red Bull's owner, congratulates Max after his victory in the 2018 Austrian Grand Prix.

This is the 'steering wheel' that faced Max in 2016 when he first raced
a Red Bull — now, just a few years later, the design has developed
to an even higher level of sophistication and complexity.

problems with his. He stepped into the Red Bull RB12 as if it were an ordinary day at the office, even if the interior décor and the furniture had changed. He immediately found the light switch and took his seat at the head of the boardroom table.

In Formula 1, drivers don't often change seats during the season. There's a reason for that. Changing cars is different from a transfer to another football team. It is — just to mention it — life-threatening. If, in the heat of the moment, a driver falls back on a routine that has become ingrained and suddenly changes, the consequences can be severe. Moreover, a car is partly personalised. The seat has to be made-to-measure, to name but one aspect.

Normally, a driver switches teams during the long winter break and his new team has plenty of time to adjust its car to his dimensions and preferences. The new driver in turn has a few months to get used to his new driving environment — mainly in the simulator but also in the limited testing permitted these days.

It wasn't like that for Max Verstappen. He had only a few days to get used to the RB12 and all its differences.

The sightlines on the track with the lower nose, the balance, the electronics, the steering — these were just some of the aspects that were new. Not to mention the steering wheel, with its multiplicity of buttons and settings. Although many of these were largely the same as those of the Toro Rosso, there were differences. Differences that can easily be overlooked at 200mph in the heat of the moment.

The impressive steering wheel — actually it can no longer be called a wheel — is perhaps the component that has undergone the greatest development in recent years. Who remembers the brave pioneers who raced their Silver Arrows around the Nürburgring? Their steering wheels were as big as the actual wheels. Like every component in a modern Formula 1 car, the steering wheel is a technical masterpiece that pushes and perhaps stretches the limits of human response.

Comparing a Formula 1 driver with the pilot of a fighter jet isn't far-fetched. It's appropriate that the drivers in Formula 1 are increasingly referred to as pilots. Not only do they need absolute mastery of their cars, but they must also deal with all the demands of the track itself, where wheel-to-wheel racing requires incredible judgement and split-second reactions. It isn't unlike a dogfight between fighter planes at war.

The Flying Dutchman had no problems with it. The ease with which he mastered the Red Bull RB12 attracted worldwide admiration. Red Bull Racing team principal Christian Horner was at a loss for words.

'He was so calm at the end of the race, in control. Very impressive, and he'll only get stronger as he gets to know the car better and his confidence increases,' Horner said afterwards.

'He did not,' the boss added, 'make a single mistake.'

There used to be active telemetry from the pits to the cars, allowing remote adjustments to be made during a race, but the FIA felt this was becoming a bridge too far. If the cars are going to be controlled from the pits, the drivers can be done away with too — that was the governing body's stance. With active telemetry, Formula 1 was just one step away from a competition between self-driving cars.

For example, it would be technically easy to activate the Drag Reduction System (DRS) from the garage. This is the system whereby the rear wing opens to create less downforce, allowing the car to pass thanks to a burst of extra speed. For racing purists, this is artificial and strange. A driver can, they say, defend his position in corners for all he's worth, but he's put at a substantial disadvantage if a rival uses the DRS.

Control from the pits disappeared in 2008 with the requirement for all teams to use a standard Electronic Control Unit (ECU), the car's brain, as supplied by McLaren Electronic Systems. One consequence was to accelerate the development of the steering wheel. Although there were already quite a lot of buttons and controls on a Formula 1 steering wheel, they have proliferated since 2008 to the point where there are now more than 30, some of which have multiple functions. In total, the driver has about 50 settings to manage, ranging from the drink button to the speed limiter that gets activated in the pitlane.

Nowadays, therefore, the engineer gives an instruction by radio to the driver, who can then do as he's asked — or not — using the controls on the steering wheel. The only partial exception is the DRS, which still has a telemetric aspect in that it's enabled remotely but the driver chooses when to activate it.

A Formula 1 car has a limited form of power steering, using hydraulic assistance alone, but its effect shouldn't be overestimated. Due to the enormous downforce, wide tyres and the small size of the steering wheel, a driver's arm movements when steering are quite small but need significant strength.

Damon Hill, the 1996 World Champion, had a special fitness machine designed for this purpose so that he could keep his neck and forearms strong during the winter.

The data harvesting of Formula 1 cars is phenomenal. Each car has about 120 sensors — the precise number varies from circuit to circuit — that continually gather information. From oil pressure to cooling, from tyre temperature to G-forces, even the driver's heart rate. The data is gathered and stored in the ECU and from there, via the telemetry antenna, reaches the team's engineers, many of whom will be at base rather than at the race itself, sometimes on the other side of the world. The information is calculated and shared with the driver, who can change his car's behaviour through the settings on the steering wheel.

In the digital age, therefore, the engineer can see exactly where the driver has made a mistake or could do things better. Almost perversely, the advent of the computer has considerably increased the driver's workload.

The steering wheel of Max's Red Bull has 12 push buttons in different colours and seven adjustable dials. Then there are the flippers for the gears, which are used about 4,000 times during a race, and for the clutch, which the driver only operates manually at a race start. There's even a control for tracks that turn anti-clockwise, as is the case in Abu Dhabi, Azerbaijan, Brazil, Singapore and the United States.

The driver's finger movements are almost innumerable. The complex steering wheel adds another dimension to the profession of Formula 1 driver. Mercedes driver Lewis Hamilton, who was closely involved in the development of his car's new steering wheel for the 2016 season, said: 'It's an incredibly complicated piece of kit. There's so much information on it, it took me the whole winter break to get the hang of it.'

When Max Verstappen was elevated to the Red Bull team, he had just a few days to understand his new steering wheel. It's yet another indication of how quickly he developed as a Formula 1 driver. The kart in which he had celebrated his triumphs a few years earlier didn't have a single button on its steering wheel.

CHAPTER 18
TEAM-MATES

When Max Verstappen lost a podium finish at the 2017 United States Grand Prix in Austin due to intervention by Australian steward Garry Connelly, he reacted furiously. On the last lap of the race, the then 20-year-old driver passed Kimi Räikkönen's Ferrari in a do-or-die attempt to get on the podium, but in doing so he contravened regulations by gaining an advantage from briefly putting all four wheels outside the boundary of the track marked by white lines.

He was given a five-second time penalty and therefore was classified fourth instead of third. His reaction was understandably emotional. Drivers are pumped with adrenaline when they cross the finish line of a Grand Prix. If a hard-won prize is then taken away after a dispassionate intervention by a judge, a reaction is understandable. Especially when asked, as Verstappen was, to leave the Cooldown Room to make way for Räikkönen.

It was undoubtedly a humiliating experience. That cooling-off area, where cameras used to observe the top three drivers after a race, could sometimes be a battlefield, where disgruntled racers exchange stern glances or studiously avoid each other. It often made for compelling viewing, even if nowadays, due to the pandemic, it's no longer a feature of the television menu.

In the world of global top-class sport, courteous, sociable behaviour is almost a requirement, because so many of a driver's actions are under the magnifying glass of the media. Verstappen had to find a way to deal with this. Middle ground had to be found between, on the one side, the blunt honesty and impolite tendency of a typical Dutchman coupled with Verstappen DNA, and, on the other side, the requisite charm and charisma of a role model.

Lewis Hamilton has become a master at this over the years. After he was reviled by the Orange Army following the clash at Silverstone in 2021, the reigning World Champion launched an unparalleled charm offensive. On the first day of the Dutch Grand Prix, he appeared in an orange-coloured outfit, topped off with bright orange sunglasses. It was an ode to the Netherlands in general and the Orange Army in particular. This all worked so well that he managed to take the sting out of Holland's hatred. At Zandvoort, the booing that had marred proceedings a few weeks earlier in Hungary was barely heard. Instead, the reigning World Champion drew applause and admiration in the lion's den. Moreover, when it was all over he praised the race winner, Max Verstappen, to the skies, thus wrapping the Dutch fans around his little finger.

Due to his youth, it's fair to say that Verstappen was cut some slack in his early seasons, and allowed to be perhaps too self-centred, and to behave at times in a somewhat unseemly way. His youthful open-mindedness acted as a shield against criticism, but by observing Lewis Hamilton and Sebastian Vettel he gradually came round. The team, his mechanics and the fans received their share of appreciation in return. He thanked them for services rendered and involved them in the party after a success. He didn't do himself any harm by doing that.

Without losing any of his appealing spontaneity, he grew into his exemplary position as a Formula 1 superstar, without suffering from self-regard. As Bruce Springsteen once so aptly described it: 'Don't take yourself too seriously, and take yourself as seriously as death itself.'

And that's how Max comes across now. In the glamorous make-believe world of Formula 1, it's all too tempting to lose yourself in hubris. Although the authenticity remained, the tone gradually changed. Verstappen became increasingly aware of the impact of his words, without losing their power.

Journalist David Tremayne: 'He doesn't share more than he wants to, doesn't waste any more words than strictly necessary. Why talk so much? I love his media appearances. He always looks interested and in that respect I think he's a bit like Seb [Sebastian Vettel], who's prepared to think about the question before answering. He's honest and straightforward and comfortable on the big stage.'

In Formula 1, primal reactions are part of the entertainment. The on-board radio, which is now on a time delay and sometimes censored because many drivers swear rather readily when provoked, adds extra entertainment value to the race. Not only because of the technical information, but also the emotion that can pour from the drivers' voices.

Verstappen is well aware that the radio records everything and uses this as an extra weapon in the hunt for success. Kimi Räikkönen was the undisputed king of one-liners. Lewis Hamilton issues excuses when things go wrong, complaining about tyres, about strategy, about the car. When venting his anger at another driver, Max's favourite phrase has been 'What an idiot' or, a little more trenchantly, 'What a moron', preceded or followed by censored bleeps.

Helmut Marko describes the radio behaviour of his protégé as unique — because Max is always available to speak. Whereas other drivers usually save their comments for straight stretches of track, 'Max has so much space available in his mind that he also uses the radio in the corners.'

In his early years, Verstappen was a gift to Formula 1's entertainment value. Liberty Media, the American owner of Formula 1, has done everything it can to popularise the sport since its takeover in 2017. In particular, the interaction between fans and the sport has exploded through social media. The on-board radio provides interesting content for this.

With his heart on his sleeve, the young Dutchman expresses the unfiltered emotions that every sportsman feels, but not everyone conveys so directly. And that works, as his voice begins to have more and more influence. In 2019, Verstappen accused Ferrari of cheating, after which the Scuderia found itself under the spotlight. When the Ferraris were suddenly a lot slower in Texas, he rubbed more salt in the wound by saying, 'That's what happens when you stop cheating.'

Hmmm... for a moment it seemed as if echoes of Senna had returned. The Brazilian, proclaimed by many to be the best driver ever, never minced his words either. Senna took everyone — including the corrupt Jean-Marie Balestre who headed Formula 1's governing body — to task when necessary. After a good few years in Formula 1 with a top team, Verstappen now knows the weight of words.

Returning to the 2017 United States Grand Prix, David Tremayne spoke to the steward responsible for the five-second penalty issued to Verstappen after consultation with the other two judges, Radovan Novak and Mika Salo. The

Daniel Ricciardo, Max's first Red Bull team-mate, congratulates
the new boy after his victory in Spain in 2016.

repercussions were pretty hard on Connelly, even if Verstappen soon got over it and prepared himself for the next race.

Tremayne: 'Connelly gave me a letter with the arguments for the infringement and the punishment, an explanation of why they did what they did. I gave that letter to Max and later I asked him if he'd read it. He hadn't. He'd thrown it away, because he knew what was in it anyway. I found that striking, because I've seen many youngsters in Formula 1 who couldn't even string together a few words. Not because they couldn't do it, or — even worse — because they were boring, but because they were scared to death to speak out. Max has never been afraid of that. That's good, because you need people who dare to speak out.

'Sometimes what comes out is a bit blunt, or direct, and you don't agree with it, but I think it's great that he does it. Even though he has become more careful with his statements, it's still nice to see that honesty. He's tough on other competitors and rivals, but he makes the sport exciting. Formula 1 needed someone who believes in himself completely. It works on other fronts too. He has a whole team behind him who support him. And his fans love it too.'

Others have preceded him in letting emotions spill over. At the 1998 Belgian Grand Prix, while leading in torrential rain and limited visibility, Michael Schumacher went into the back of David Coulthard's McLaren while lapping it. When he returned to the pits, he stormed over to the McLaren garage to vent his fury at the Scottish driver and had to be restrained by some of the bystanders.

In Brazil in 2018, as we saw at the beginning of this book, Verstappen was on his way to an uncontested win when Esteban Ocon, who was a lap down, drove him off the track. Rather like Schumacher 20 years earlier, the aggrieved Dutchman, denied his victory, tried to pick a fight with Ocon during the weigh-in afterwards. Unable or unwilling to restrain himself, Verstappen gave the Frenchman a piece of his mind and shoved him several times.

Tremayne: 'Yes, there's aggression. But that's exactly what the sport needs. He has also been hard on Charles Leclerc and Lewis Hamilton. He goes for it, whatever it takes. His style is powerful and always attacking — why not? If I watch five minutes of an England football match, I quickly get bored, because they always seem to pass the ball backwards. Max never stops pushing. Especially in his early seasons, he didn't care how many times he crashed. And he always comes out stronger.

'One of my favourite sports quotes of all time is from boxer Jack Dempsey: "A champion is someone who gets up when he can't." Lewis Hamilton is like that. Max is cut from the same cloth.'

Verstappen hasn't always realised the impact of an ill-chosen word, as in free practice for the 2020 Portuguese Grand Prix when he called Lance Stroll a 'retard' and a 'mongol' after a collision. The latter word — an out-of-date term for someone with Down syndrome — caused widespread offence, prompting the Mongol Identity organisation to release a letter expressing its 'disgust and deep concern'. He never apologised but he did say a few words about it: 'It happened in the heat of the moment. I didn't mean anything by it. Apparently we live in a world where everything is perhaps a little sensitive.'

He certainly attracts attention with his comments, whether plain offensive or more commonly just politically incorrect. His actions, words and driving style are controversial at times and arouse admiration and sometimes disgust too. It's mostly an attractive characteristic when a sportsman is 'always going for it'. That Verstappen pushes the limits is part of the job.

Max Verstappen has devoured his team-mates whole. Certainly Daniel Ricciardo, another of Helmut Marko's protégés, ended up crushed by the Dutchman. He fled — for a lot of money — to Renault, knowing that at Red Bull the cards had been dealt and he didn't have a winning hand. Verstappen had developed into the undisputed number one.

Initially, Ricciardo was able to keep up but the rivalry between the team-mates came to a tremendous explosion in 2018 in Azerbaijan, where they drove each other out of the race. Ricciardo was so angry that he wanted to throw his helmet at his team-mate. He showed why he's nicknamed 'The Honey Badger' — an animal that, in the cheerful Australian's words, 'seems quite cute and cuddly, but as soon as someone crosses his territory in a way he doesn't like, he turns into a bit of a savage'.

Like many conflicts in Formula 1, however, the bitterness soon faded. In the end, the drivers had too much respect and friendship for each other to let things escalate any further.

For a long time Ayrton Senna was Alain Prost's worst enemy. The two fought tooth and nail on the track and were never friends off it. But even before Senna's death, the enmity evolved into respect and admiration. At Senna's funeral in Brazil, Prost was one of the pall-bearers.

Sergio Pérez proved to be the perfect team-mate throughout 2021,
right down to his role in duelling with Lewis Hamilton during
the season-ending Abu Dhabi Grand Prix.

At the end of that 2018 season, Ricciardo left Red Bull. Although once seen by Helmut Marko as a potential World Champion and possible successor to Sebastian Vettel, he never lived up to that expectation. In going to another team, Renault, he traded his World Championship ambitions for occasional successes, achieving no more than two third places in his two years with the French team.

The first driver you have to beat in Formula 1 is your team-mate. Verstappen has always done that. Little by little, his team-mates have been marginalised, relegated to extras on the set. First there was Carlos Sainz Jr at Toro Rosso, then Ricciardo was followed at Red Bull by Pierre Gasly, Alexander Albon and Sergio Pérez. Even Pérez, a well-established driver whom Red Bull values highly, had to accept the role of number two, never able to threaten the number one.

Of all of them, Ricciardo has left the biggest impression, and not just because of his qualities as a driver. Verstappen may have got under the Aussie's skin but they became the best of friends.

Journalist Will Buxton: 'I think the relationship with Daniel when they were team-mates brought Max a lot. He saw how Daniel looked at the world and approached it. How he could have fun and not have to take everything so seriously all the time. When Daniel puts on his helmet, he's dead serious. But when he takes off his helmet, he can laugh, make jokes — and that worked well with Max.

'You sometimes saw Max looking at him with those big brotherly eyes that radiated eagerness to learn. I think he learned from Daniel how to turn himself off. Max was always on. If he wasn't in the car, then he was behind the simulator. All he has done in his life is race. That can make for a very boring, one-sided life if you don't have any fun or passion on the side. I think Max has learned from all the people around him to broaden his scope. That's helped to make him a better driver.

'With the next guys who joined the team, Gasly and Albon, the relationship was completely different. He saw himself as superior to them, which was true, and therefore couldn't learn anything from them. All the steps he has taken have helped to strengthen his personality. He got older, got to know more people, and learned from them.

'When we're 19, we think we know everything, don't we? We think the world owes us a living, that it revolves around us. But then you get into your 20s and think back and realise you were just a kid. But then you turn 30 and

Having seen the media demands placed on Daniel Ricciardo at the Aussie's home race, Max approached the Dutch Grand Prix in 2021 with detachment and focus amidst the orange fervour.

think back to your 20s and you think: boy, I didn't really know anything back then.

'After his victory in Austria in 2021, I said to Max that this was the best we have seen from him. He replied: "Oh no, that won't happen until I'm 30." He has become aware that you don't need to have everything here and now. He used to want everything yesterday. Now he appreciates that the best is yet to come. That you cannot suddenly invent maturity or experience, but that it comes to you if you're willing to learn, in life and in racing. And Max is learning his lessons. Every day.'

The uncomplicated and good-humoured Ricciardo is one of the most experienced drivers in Formula 1. He has won a good few Grands Prix — seven during his Red Bull years — but never his home race in Melbourne. In fact, he has never even stood on the podium down under and the chances of that happening aren't getting any stronger. This has hurt, as he revealed in his own podcast.

'It's just too busy at a home Grand Prix. Everyone wants something from you and you want to disappoint as few people as possible. I tried to please everyone, but I forgot myself.'

This brings us neatly to an example of a lesson learned from 'The Honey Badger'. It was a madhouse at Zandvoort in 2021, the first Dutch Grand Prix in 36 years. With the *Jumbo Racedagen* now a thing of the past, this was the only opportunity for Dutch fans to see their hero on home soil. An enormous cloud of orange smoke enveloped the circuit, drifting slowly up the North Sea on that sunny, windless weekend. Verstappen fever had never been so intense.

The consequence could have been too much distraction. After all, everyone wanted a bit of Max now, to talk to him, photograph him, film him — shake his hand or get a selfie if possible. The flattery was totally wasted on him. He approached the weekend as if the race were taking place in a desert, far away from partisan emotions. His focus wasn't diverted by all the attention and adulation.

'I saw how Daniel did it in his home race. He did a lot of media things there and we didn't do that here. Everyone knows that by now, because I have been very clear about that. So it really depends on how you prepare.'

How he did prepare was with total focus. The run-up to the Grand Prix gave the whole of the Netherlands sleepless nights — except for Max Verstappen. The protagonist's only distraction was to give the Dutch king and consort a brief guided tour of Red Bull's garage an hour before the race.

Verstappen won. Royally. From pole position to chequered flag. The 23-year-old who felt the pressure of the entire nation on his shoulders didn't go off the boil for a moment. His flawless start was followed by an immaculate race. On a track that was his own, where he had won in Formula 3 and had been fêted at spectacular demonstration days, where he must have felt like he was in seventh heaven, he did what his fans hoped and expected. He remained resolutely calm, focused on one goal: winning. Even during the emotional singing of the national anthem, he kept his cool.

As for his father, it was as if Jos the Boss had carried the weight of the nation for his son. Jos wasn't even there to see Max's victory. Perhaps overcome by nerves or tension, he had developed severe abdominal pain and had been taken to hospital, where nothing amiss was found.

The Verstappens, as the Netherlands knows, will do anything to win.

Australian journalist Peter Windsor, whose racing hero was Jim Clark, likened Verstappen's performance at Zandvoort to Clark at his best: 'A brilliant start. As early as the first lap, he built up a gap with a full tank and then consolidated it. It looks easy, but only works with a top car and a top driver.'

And, in terms of atmosphere, Windsor measured the occasion against the home successes of Nigel Mansell and Lewis Hamilton at Silverstone, and others elsewhere: 'Like Carlos Reutemann in Argentina, Clay Regazzoni at Monza, but 20 times bigger.'

If Verstappen's 2016 victory at Barcelona was proof of his immense talent, the 2021 season — with all its turmoil, controversies, highs and lows, crashes and narrow escapes — opened the door to the future. He had won races before, fought duels and won, but now he became the equal of Lewis Hamilton, and Red Bull nearly became the equal of Mercedes. Now there were no more excuses as the season boiled down to an astonishingly intense duel between the two best drivers and teams in Formula 1. On one track one had the advantage, on the next the other. Some familiar patterns also changed under Verstappen's pressure: Monza, Ferrari's home track, had normally suited Mercedes, but not in 2021.

Windsor compares the Max of today with 'his' Nigel of yesterday. Mansell, the 1992 World Champion with Williams. Mansell, the uncompromising British hero worshipped by the masses in his home country, the man who asked the chef in a starred restaurant if he could have ketchup with his chateaubriand.

'One of the reasons Max does such a good job with this car is his experience. He has driven a lot of Grands Prix, excellent races in which he often finished third or fourth. When you have driven a whole series of races like that and you find yourself in a very good car, winning becomes incredibly logical and easy. I say this because I worked with Nigel for a long time, and he ate more dirt than Max ever did. Nigel drove really bad cars before he ended up in the Williams that gave him the world title.

'One of the reasons Nigel was so good in the Williams was that he could drive incredibly fast in poor cars. He never gave up, even if it was eighth place. He always drove 100 percent and that's exactly what Max is doing now. Even when Max didn't find himself in the top three, he fought for every spot, in every corner. Anyone who claims that Max is a different driver now, that he has matured, doesn't know what they're talking about.

'Nothing has changed except that he has more mileage behind him and is in a better car. What's more, Red Bull has managed to build a car around him that he can get 100 per cent out of, whereas others only get 95 per cent. It's also great for Adrian Newey to be able to build a car for a driver like Max Verstappen. With drivers like David Coulthard or Daniel Ricciardo you never know where you will end up. With Max you do.'

In Australia in 2015, aged just 17, Max Verstappen was thrown in at the deep end and swam confidently to the other side.

'With Max,' concludes Will Buxton, 'everything fell into place on his début. In a single year he went through primary school, secondary school and university. His learning curve was steeper than the Matterhorn. He learned everything at once. He had to. He drove in a team that doesn't offer second chances and doesn't tolerate excuses. But Max didn't require any second chances and didn't need to make any excuses.'

CHAPTER 19
MEMORABLE RACES

To come up with any review of a driver's finest races is always going to be somewhat arbitrary. My selection for Max Verstappen may seem rather random but there are a few patterns. Brazil, for example, features strongly: in the five times Max raced at Interlagos, from 2015 to 2019, he hit the spot three times, although only his last visit brought victory. Austria is very much a favourite for him: he has won four times at the Red Bull Ring in front of the annual invasion of the Orange Army. Mexico is another good stamping ground, with three wins there. And into 2021, Zandvoort has been added — and even Monaco too.

The Dutch Grand Prix of 2021, of course, was a high point in Verstappen's career. The race itself wasn't that memorable because he was so dominant, but the enormity of the occasion and the intensity of the emotions — with Zandvoort back on the calendar after 36 years and a Dutchman winning — provided incredible joy for his fans and, indeed, his grateful nation.

Maybe his first victory in Barcelona should be judged one of his best performances. There was a time when he himself thought so, but not anymore, because Nico Rosberg and Lewis Hamilton eliminated each other on the first lap and without the usual Mercedes opposition he only had to battle with Kimi Räikkönen's Ferrari.

Very high on the list of Max Verstappen's finest races must be the 2016 Brazilian Grand Prix. The penultimate race of his first season as a Red Bull driver, it underlined his qualities as a driver of the future, in the homeland of Ayrton Senna on the capricious Interlagos circuit.

It was raining hard. Choice of tyres was automatically 'full wets', which can displace 85 litres of water per second per wheel at 300kph (186mph). That's vital on this circuit, where puddles form in heavy rain, lurking like booby traps.

It was one of those days with tension in the air, like the period between lightning and thunder. After the flash there's silence, but then inevitably comes the clap, sometimes so loud and immediate that it seems to rip the air apart, but at other times muffled and distant.

You could almost smell the tension at Interlagos, with rain, rubber and fuel forming a unique cocktail of scents that sharpened the senses.

The atmosphere was redolent of 2008, when Lewis Hamilton snatched his first world title from the jaws of defeat, at the last corner of the last lap, with an overtaking move that secured fifth place and gave him a crucial extra championship point. Felipe Massa, the local hero, won the race and thought he was World Champion, but had to acknowledge defeat tearfully. That's how cruel top sport is. That's how cruel Interlagos is.

The focus at the 2016 race was once again on Hamilton, this time because of his World Championship battle with Mercedes team-mate and rival Nico Rosberg. Hamilton won the race, thereby keeping alive his chances of claiming the title at the finale in Abu Dhabi, where Rosberg duly secured the crown. At Interlagos, however, there was more admiration for Max Verstappen than for either of the Mercedes men.

In the run-up to the race, the weather looked threatening. Dark clouds hung over the track like a pile of wet towels.

Rain is the great equaliser in motor racing. When it rains, the outcome is no longer about budgets, engine power or strategies. It's much more about the driver. Only the very best can truly perform in the rain: Ayrton Senna, Michael Schumacher… and Lewis Hamilton. Rosberg never liked it. He became anxious, especially under pressure.

Any normal person would be terrified. Spray from the tyres almost completely obscures a pursuing driver's view. He sees only the flashing red light on the back of the car in front and has to drive almost blind. These gladiators require total faith in each other.

All pre-planned strategies can be discarded. Ideally, the drivers can race to the finish without pitstops if nothing changes. But something always happens in races under these conditions. Nothing is predictable.

At Interlagos in 2016, Bernd Mayländer's safety car had to lead the field away because a standing start was too dangerous. To use a favourite Hamilton phrase, it was 'hammer time'. To illustrate how tricky the conditions were, Romain Grosjean crashed his Haas car on the way to the grid. Renault driver Jolyon Palmer described the conditions tellingly: 'I could only see my own steering wheel.'

There was so much incident. When Kimi Räikkönen crashed after 19 laps, 14 of which had been run behind the safety car, the race was red-flagged. The restart took place behind the safety car in worsening conditions and after seven more laps of procession the race was stopped again. Only after another restart was the Brazilian Grand Prix able to run its course.

Racing in the rain is a gift to Max Verstappen. When karting, he used to go out when it was wet for extra practice. At Interlagos, the conditions were ideal for him. Totally and utterly soaking. For the entire race. It just kept on raining.

Near the end, the rain showed signs of easing and the Red Bull team decided to gamble. The full wets were taken off and intermediates fitted. If it were to become drier, Max could make up lots of time and maybe even win. The gamble went wrong. The rain fell harder and Max pressed for another pitstop to go back to proper wets. 'I feel like I'm driving a boat,' he said over the radio. His team heeded the call for help and brought him in. He returned to the track in 16th place, with 17 laps to go.

But now he's unleashed. His overtaking is incredible, on the inside, on the outside, whatever's best. At one point, through the fast left-hander leading onto the start/finish straight, he very nearly loses it when the rear of the car swings round 90 degrees. His rescue is breathtaking. As in the choreography of Swan Lake, he controls the Red Bull's slide, locking and releasing the wheels with exquisite timing. The car's nose returns to the right direction just before the crash barrier and, as if nothing has happened, the driver continues his mission. From the pits, his race engineer coolly says: 'Well held Max, well held.'

As the laps are counted down, he slices through the points-scoring positions. One by one he makes the passes stick... Valtteri Bottas, Daniel Ricciardo, Carlos Sainz Jr, Sebastian Vettel. Now he's fourth, with third-placed Sergio Pérez's Force India in sight. This last one is the best of all. Not only does

Max showed everyone else how to do it in the 2016 Brazilian Grand Prix. In the last 17 laps, in soaking conditions, he sliced through the field from 16th place to third.

Pérez offer stubborn resistance, but the distance Verstappen must make up just before he pounces is enormous. He applies the brakes incredibly late. There's no uncertainty. The overtaking manoeuvre is accurate and decisive.

When the race is finally over, Verstappen is third. A deafening cheer breaks out. The Dutchman is the talk of the town. He's lauded all over the world. This is Senna all over again. Formula 1 has a new hero.

Max's achievement even surprises Jos, who receives congratulations on his son's behalf. Niki Lauda comes up and doffs his ever-present cap. Jos, still recovering from the shock, says: 'I've seen a lot of him, but this was incredible.'

Of course, Max himself enjoys the compliments, all smiles. Asked by British reporter Lee McKenzie how he came to be so good in the rain, he answers wryly: 'I'm Dutch.'

Red Bull's collaboration with Honda was a calculated gamble when it began in 2019, even if everyone at the team was relieved to end the use of Renault power. After all, the deteriorating relationship with Red Bull's long-standing French engine supplier had become one of the most talked-about topics of the Formula 1 paddock. Renault's Cyril Abiteboul had become so fed up with the stream of complaint from Christian Horner and his drivers, especially Max Verstappen, that he had 'stopped reading comments' from the Red Bull camp as early as 2015. How could it have come to this?

Renault and Red Bull had enjoyed an intimate and enduring love affair that had brought a great deal of glory. The relationship began in 2007, one year after the creation of the Red Bull Formula 1 team, and quickly blossomed. The victories started to arrive in 2009 and the following year brought the first of four consecutive World Championship crowns for Sebastian Vettel and constructors' titles for the team. The combination of Red Bull, Renault and Vettel was almost unbeatable. That sustained spell of success delivered 47 Grand Prix wins in the 2009–13 period.

The introduction of hybrid V6 turbocharged power units in 2014 brought the first cracks in the partnership. Compared with Mercedes and Ferrari, Renault had considerable difficulty in getting to grips with the complex new technology, putting the Red Bull team at a considerable disadvantage. Achieving both speed and reliability proved to be a tough challenge for the French engine supplier in the hybrid era.

By 2015, frustrations were running so high that Red Bull owner Dietrich Mateschitz threatened to leave Formula 1 if the engine problem wasn't resolved.

The team went looking elsewhere for engines for the 2016 season. First on the list was Mercedes and talks were held before the German company said 'no'. Ferrari — supplier of engines to Toro Rosso at that time — did express willingness to help, but the Scuderia had no desire to equip the best chassis in Formula 1 with an up-to-date engine and only offered a 2015-specification version. For Red Bull's ambitious leadership, that wasn't an option. So, the increasingly fractious relationship with Renault continued.

So much went wrong with the Renault engine at the start of 2017 that Horner was at a loss, especially as no alternatives were available. He had slammed the door on the possibility of Mercedes engines, as team boss Toto Wolff revealed: 'They [Red Bull] express themselves so negatively about a partner that we don't see any future together. Formula 1 is like private life. It's about compromise and recognising your partner's strengths and weaknesses, and helping each other.'

This loss of form at Red Bull very much compromised Max Verstappen's first three seasons with the team. His criticism of the Renault engine, indeed, became so stark that divorce was unavoidable. The Dutchman didn't mince his words and was quick to comment every time there was an engine failure or he lacked power.

The lows were more notable than the highs. The sports motto 'you win together and lose together' certainly didn't apply to the Red Bull/Renault combination during Max's time. Of course, in the context of this chapter — a look at his finest races — it affected what he could achieve on the track, although we must keep this in perspective. He still looked mightily impressive against all yardsticks.

With 81 starts using Renault power, Max won five times and retired 10 times. In the same period, team-mate Daniel Ricciardo won four times and retired 14 times. For both drivers, the most frequent causes of retirement were technical failures in the electrical systems of the hybrid power unit.

Red Bull's reliability woes were at their worst in 2018: that year Lewis Hamilton, the World Champion, suffered only one technical failure, in Austria due to loss of oil pressure, whereas Red Bull's drivers had 12 between them.

In everybody's judgement, including Verstappen's, that Austrian Grand Prix brought his finest performance of 2018. After starting from fourth on the grid, he was soon in charge. This was the race in which he and Red Bull showed that the potential to battle with the top teams and win was still there. An added treat for his fans, massed in their orange-coloured grandstand,

Struggles with Renault engines characterised Max's early seasons with Red Bull
but the Austrian Grand Prix of 2018, his best race of the year, brought welcome
respite — and in front of his travelling Dutch fans too.

The 2019 Austrian Grand Prix not only marked Red Bull's first victory with Honda power but also provided a stunning last-gasp duel with Charles Leclerc's Ferrari.

came when he overtook Kimi Räikkönen's Ferrari right in front of them. No wonder he declared this victory at the time to be his best yet, although he added that the best race was yet to come. How right he was.

Red Bull's relationship with Honda began in 2019. On the back of three terrible years with McLaren, the Japanese engine partner was determined to make a success of its new collaboration, with no expense or effort spared in producing a competitive engine. However, there were doubts and risks. Honda's reputation had taken a battering after the McLaren fiasco and the company's glittering history in Formula 1 was so far in the past that success certainly couldn't be taken for granted. Nevertheless, the Japanese quickly developed a strong bond with the Red Bull team and especially with Max Verstappen, who even visited the Honda factory. The new engines were warmly welcomed in Milton Keynes and lovingly integrated into Adrian Newey's chassis. This healthy relationship was based on mutual respect and, above all, a common goal — to win the World Championship.

That target looked very distant at the outset. Mercedes and Ferrari had more power, speed, and experience. But that changed as the 2019 season wore on, starting with the Austrian Grand Prix. At the Red Bull Ring, Max Verstappen achieved a fantastic victory. It was Honda's first for 13 years.

It was a spectacular performance — a taste of what was to come. From second on the grid, Max made a dreadful start, the engine seeming to stall momentarily, and fell back a long way, to eighth place. Now it was time to play catch-up. After 50 laps of the 71, though, he was still only fourth — but then he resumed his charge to the front in earnest. On that lap he passed Sebastian Vettel's Ferrari. Six laps later he dealt with Valtteri Bottas's Mercedes. And with three laps to go he was all over Charles Leclerc's Ferrari. The wheel-to-wheel jousting was nerve-wracking, with 18,000 Dutch fans in their special grandstand on the edges of their seats. Verstappen kept up the attack for a full lap until he dealt his rival the decisive blow with a gentle wheel bang while claiming the corner. Could that massive orange support have squeezed out the last drop of his attacking spirit? Could some form of home advantage have played a part?

But the most wonderful gesture was yet to come. On his way to the top step of the podium, Verstappen straightened his race suit, smiled broadly and pointed both forefingers at the Honda logo on his chest. The Japanese engine manufacturer appreciated that almost as much as the victory itself. Honda was back and many more successes would follow.

After that victory in Austria, the British Grand Prix at Silverstone followed two weeks later. Silverstone is part of Britain's cultural heritage, inextricably entwined in motor racing history as the venue for the very first Formula 1 World Championship race way back in 1950. Many of today's corner names — Copse, Maggots, Becketts, Chapel, Stowe, Club, Abbey and Woodcote -- go right back to the circuit's birth. With eight British Grand Prix victories at Silverstone, Lewis Hamilton, too, has become a folk hero in his country, as recognised by his knighthood in 2021.

At Silverstone in 2019 Verstappen was the star of the show, even though he never led. He crossed swords again with Charles Leclerc. On the 14th lap of the race, the third-placed Ferrari and the fourth-placed Red Bull went into the pits for new tyres at the same time, Leclerc in front. This was a moment when hundredths of a second would count and Red Bull's crew was a fraction quicker than Ferrari's. The protagonists drove out of the pitlane literally wheel-to-wheel, with Verstappen on the right and therefore with the advantage into the sharp right-hander after the pitlane exit. When their man passed his Ferrari rival, Red Bull's mechanics slapped each other on the shoulders and exchanged high fives. Their cheers were premature. Verstappen made a rare mistake at the very next corner and ran slightly wide, allowing Leclerc to repass.

The British TV commentator cried out in astonishment: 'Has all the good work [of the pit crew] become undone?' But the duel continued and a few laps later he added: 'This is absolutely brilliant racing between two supremely talented drivers.' And then just before the halfway mark: 'How many more laps of action can Max Verstappen and Charles Leclerc give us — hopefully another 27.'

It was indeed a tense and prolonged battle, the Dutchman again fractionally the stronger. It was an undoubted highlight of the year, even if in the end Verstappen's race was ruined by Sebastian Vettel. On lap 38, running close behind Verstappen, the German braked late and ran his Ferrari into the back of the Red Bull, sending it into the gravel. 'What the fuck,' the Dutchman shouted. 'What did he do?'

It was the end of Verstappen's podium hopes, although he did get back on the track to finish fifth. At the end of the year he was given a prize anyway — the FIA's 'Action of the Year' award as voted for by fans.

Only two more weeks passed before an unforgettable German Grand Prix at Hockenheim. It was hailed as the finest contest of the season and Verstappen won it.

Bernie Ecclestone, the long-time Formula 1 boss, once floated the idea, albeit mischievously, of installing trackside water sprinklers and turning them on at unexpected moments to add to the spectacle. The damp German Grand Prix needed no such enhancement: it was one of those races where the spectators, whether at the circuit or on television, didn't know where to look to keep track of everything and even the commentators sometimes didn't know what exactly was happening. Safety cars, spins, slides, collisions, panicky tyre changes — but in all the chaos there was one driver who kept a remarkably cool head.

But even Verstappen had one indiscretion. On the 26th lap, soon after receiving slick tyres because the rain was easing, he had a big slide, rather like the one in Brazil in 2016. Once again, he proved himself a master of car control, executing a neat 360-degree gyration before resuming his race. When his RB15's back end started to slip, he applied opposite-lock, stepped on the brakes for a moment, adjusted the steering and miraculously managed to keep the car out of the gravel and crash barriers.

Much of the drama occurred at Turn 16, the circuit's brutal sharpshooter of a corner leading onto the start/finish straight. It was like a skating rink and many drivers went off there. They included the imperious Mercedes of Lewis Hamilton and Valtteri Bottas, whose indiscretions left Verstappen in command.

The Dutchman won like a veteran — and like a future World Champion. He even had to make five pitstops, two of them because of his team's misjudgement in putting him on slicks too early, when the track was still too wet. He shouted into the radio that he felt as if he was was sliding all over the place.

Some victories come quite easily. Max's back-to-back wins in Mexico in 2017 and 2018 fall into this category, even if the Autodromo Hermanos Rodríguez, opened in 2015, certainly isn't a classic track.

At the start of the 2017 Mexican Grand Prix, Verstappen put himself squarely into a three-way battle with Vettel's Ferrari and Hamilton's Mercedes going into Turn 1 on the first lap. He got the better of them and grabbed the lead. Then coming out of Turn 3, Vettel knocked the back of the Red Bull with one side of his Ferrari's front wing and punctured Hamilton's right-rear tyre with the other side. That immediately put both of Max's rivals out of contention for the win. The Dutchman went on to win by a big margin, over

A new era began in Austria in 2019 with that first Honda victory and led directly to Max becoming World Champion two years later.

20 seconds in front of Bottas's Mercedes and more than half a minute ahead of Räikkönen's Ferrari.

A year later in Mexico, he picked up a record that didn't mean much to him but was nonetheless pleasing. One day earlier, he had missed out on a different record that he would have preferred — Formula 1's youngest pole-sitter. But he did become the youngest driver to win two consecutive races at the same circuit.

There was a sharp edge to his Mexican victory of 2018. During qualifying, team-mate Daniel Ricciardo robbed him of his first-ever pole position by a minuscule margin, 0.26 second, and that hurt. So much so that, out of frustration, Max gently knocked over the '2' sign marking his result that day. However, Ricciardo's hard-fought pole position turned out to be of little value to him the next day. He was slow off the mark and lost two places. Later in the race he recovered but then crashed out, making him the driver with the most non-finishes of the season (seven). That pole was the Australian's last real achievement for Red Bull Racing. Frustrated, he departed for the Renault team, having lost out to Verstappen in the fight to be top dog at Red Bull. Meanwhile, Max took the lead on the 27th lap, building it up to a good 16 seconds on Vettel at the chequered flag, and over half a minute on Räikkönen.

Two other races from his early years in Formula 1 shouldn't be overlooked. At the second race of 2017, in China, he passed nine drivers on the first lap, rising from 16th place to seventh. He enjoyed it: 'It was like playing a video game.' He finished third.

His win in Malaysia that year, only the second of his career, was so uneventful that there's almost nothing to say about it. After two overtaking moves, he took the lead on lap four and drove smoothly to the finish — just as he likes it — with a winning margin over Hamilton of over 12 seconds.

Time goes by so quickly that we have almost forgotten how young Max Verstappen performed in his first season, at Toro Rosso. Even then he managed to attract attention. With a slower car, in a smaller team with fewer opportunities, he made a big impression from time to time.

One such moment came in the 2015 Belgian Grand Prix at Spa-Francorchamps. The way he overtook Felipe Nasr's Sauber round the outside at Blanchimont was breathtakingly brutal. He himself said soberly at the time: 'I have overtaken many times, but this one was the most beautiful. Because we go more than 300kph [186mph] there. At above 300kph it's a bit more difficult to position yourself than when you're going 200kph.' Choosing to go round the outside was also something that he hadn't previously tried in Formula 1.

That move brought him the FIA's 'Action of the Year' award. Remarkably, he has won this accolade four times. The first came when he was still in Formula 3, in 2014, when his overtaking move on Antonio Giovinazzi at Imola was selected by the voting fans. He received the award again in 2016 for his pass of Nico Rosberg in Brazil. And, as we have seen, his duel with Charles Leclerc at Silverstone in 2019 was also honoured in this way.

Verstappen also scored two extraordinary results in the Toro Rosso in 2015. The first came with his seventh place in only his second Grand Prix, in Malaysia, making him the youngest-ever driver to score points in Formula 1 — and he finished ahead of his Toro Rosso team-mate and both Red Bulls. The other was the memorable race in the United States, where he came home fourth after a rained-out weekend, behind two Mercedes and one Ferrari — his best result for Red Bull's training team.

CHAPTER 20
DESERT SHOOT-OUT

As the saying goes, time flies when you're having fun. This certainly applied to the 2021 Formula 1 season of 22 races, many of them captivating to watch. Before the climax at the Abu Dhabi Grand Prix, it had been a year of relentless controversy on and off the track, with fierce clashes and crashes, and even a cancelled race (Spa) that still yielded vital championship points.

Rarely, indeed, has a season been so much about points. Even half points became important. Even every tyre change became exciting because the single point on offer for the fastest lap could turn out to be the deciding factor — and, of course, the two leading protagonists went into the final race of the season tied on points.

The season had been a momentous and tense journey. The duelling team bosses, Toto Wolff of Mercedes and Christian Horner of Red Bull, seemed almost to age before our eyes. As for the duelling drivers, the advantage in the battle for the World Championship crown passed from one to the other five times as the season progressed.

This isn't the place to discuss each and every race of 2021 because all that can be found online, so let's just focus here on the shoot-out in the desert. Those last two races — in Saudi Arabia and Abu Dhabi — were astonishing.

The pressure on the teams was enormous but the two men in the starring roles — Lewis Hamilton and Max Verstappen — kept their composure. With two races remaining, Verstappen, still only 24, had won nine races during the season compared with Hamilton's seven. He had matured into the Dutch Master of Formula 1.

All those years of racing, right back to his earliest adventures in karting, came together in those last two races of the 2021 season. It was all or nothing. Runner-up in the World Championship would admittedly be his best result so far but now he was too close to his goal to squander the opportunity. The man who finishes second is also the first loser. That's why everything was on the line during those last two weekends of the season.

Most sports fans recognise that real winners can perform under pressure. In a big tennis final, every stroke counts, even those in the first game of the first set. In Formula 1, pole position is like that. Max missed out on pole in Saudi Arabia. Hamilton had the upper hand until Verstappen went out on his flying lap at the end of the session. It was looking good until he overdid it at the very last corner and hit the wall. It was just like his big Monaco misdemeanour, the one that had so angered Helmut Marko in 2018, only this time the world title was at stake.

Did he make that error because he succumbed to pressure? He certainly blamed himself. The unfortunate outcome was that he had to start the Saudi Arabian Grand Prix from third place on the grid, behind the two Mercedes. It was far from ideal. If, amidst the tight confines of this unforgiving street circuit, Valtteri Bottas could play his supporting role well enough, Verstappen would have an uphill struggle.

It was an unforgettable race that will be watched for years to come. It had everything — because of the driver who wouldn't give up. He was the racer who couldn't accept defeat, just as he had always been.

The race can't really be described. Its theatre was of the moment and in the outcome. There was always the potential for drama around any corner and at any moment, even if it wasn't visible. Of course, there were other drivers in the race and they could make mistakes, put their cars into the barriers. Such incidents — which were responsible for one safety car period, two red flags and four virtual safety car periods — characterised this race, with fireworks between Verstappen and Hamilton following the disruptions.

These explosions of compressed tension were a feast for the fan. Added to this were lack of clarity in the regulations and inconsistency in applying them, to the point where sometimes they seemed to be interpreted on the spot. Michael Masi, the race director, became almost a household name during these desert shoot-outs. That should never be the case with referees. They

High tension in Saudi Arabia: this is the third start of the race, with Max
swooping through from third on the grid to overtake Lewis.

must apply the rules unobtrusively. At the end of 2021, all this degenerated into messy and acrimonious dispute — which isn't good for a multi-billion-dollar sport even if it's good for entertainment.

It was all because of one man. A man who, because of his upbringing and his character, doesn't care about convention. For him, it's all about winning. That applied to the entire season but doubly so in the two last races. Verstappen must have felt the extreme tension and pressure. Or perhaps he didn't? Talking to the world's media, he seemed just as calm when the world title was on the line as he had at the age of 17, when he first stepped calmly and confidently into the Toro Rosso. On the track, however, the temperature certainly rose. It was hot in any case at these desert venues but in the cars of Hamilton and Verstappen things were hotter still.

As Sir Jackie Stewart said earlier, emotions in motorsport can be dangerous. Thankfully the two protagonists kept emotions out of it. They were simply too busy for that and the race demanded too much of their attention.

Hamilton won in Jeddah. It was no longer a question of whether that was right or wrong. He won and that was the end of Verstappen's championship lead. Going into the last race, their scores were now exactly equal, right down to the half point: 369.5.

The Yas Marina circuit in Abu Dhabi has been regarded as more suited to Mercedes but this year there were no such certainties. Red Bull had closed the gap, thanks to Verstappen, who had added wings to his RB16B with his uncompromising, attacking approach. Hamilton knew that. The reigning World Champion has been through a lot in his long career but, as he has said, 'this guy is unbelievable'.

Verstappen put himself on pole in Abu Dhabi. Now the desert shoot-out became the motorsport equivalent of Muhammad Ali's legendary 1970s boxing showdowns with George Foreman (Rumble in the Jungle) and Joe Frazier (Thrilla in Manila). Massive numbers of people, not just the usual enthusiasts, watched on television, on computer screens, on tablets, on phones. And what they saw was an apparent anti-climax.

In the Netherlands, Verstappen's home fans lost heart. Was this going to be another moment of national anguish, like those three World Cup finals that had ended in defeat? Right from the beginning, when the Dutchman made a poor start and gave away his pole-position advantage, it looked like it wasn't going to be his afternoon. Not when Hamilton pulled out a seemingly unbridgeable gap nor when team-mate Sergio 'Checo' Pérez defiantly held up

High drama in Abu Dhabi: Max takes the chequered flag, Lewis trails
– vanquished on the last lap in the harshest circumstances.

the race leader and cost him a few seconds. No, the dice weren't going to roll Verstappen's way.

Five laps from the end, everything changed.

We all know what happened. Nicolas Latifi put his Alfa Romeo into the wall and the safety car came out. Verstappen took the opportunity to pit for a new set of soft tyres. The field circulated with Hamilton in front, then five backmarkers, then Verstappen. Those backmarkers were initially told by the race director to hold position, but then, after an intervention from Red Bull, they were instructed to overtake the safety car. Now Max, on fresh tyres, was right behind Lewis. Then the safety car peeled off with one lap of the race remaining.

Hamilton, on well-worn hard tyres, was a sitting duck. His carefully nurtured lead had disappeared like snow in desert sun. Suddenly everything was different. Across the Netherlands fans exploded with joy when Verstappen took the lead. In the United Kingdom they put their heads in their hands. After Verstappen passed the chequered flag, he let rip with a deafening scream inside his helmet.

Desert dust hung over the Yas Marina arena for a long time afterwards. Protests, frustrations, uncertainty.

Sir Lewis Hamilton took his defeat graciously, like a worthy sportsman. All the rivalry, which had become almost personal, was suddenly over.

For now.

He congratulated the new World Champion.

CHAPTER 21
SPEAKING HIS MIND

Max Verstappen's character shines through in the many media appearances he has made since his arrival in Formula 1. This chapter presents an anthology of quotes over the years, collected from newspapers, television appearances, press conferences and reliable online media.

- What he remembered most about his first win in Spain 2016: 'When I stood on the podium and saw my father standing at the bottom right.'
- On overtaking in 2017: 'Whether we can still overtake with these wider cars? The plan is precisely not to have to overtake anyone at all this season.'
- What he would ask of himself: 'I actually have no idea. I think I just wouldn't interview myself at all.'
- On the mental pressure: 'Worrying doesn't make you faster, so I don't.'
- Whether he thinks about his media appearances: 'I say what I want to say and am careful not to say what I don't want to.'
- About the attention paid to his private life: 'It's not so much that it bothers me, it just isn't about anything. Apparently, I have a new girlfriend every two or three weeks, which just doesn't make sense.'
- About the expectations of the outside world: 'Maybe other people are disappointed sometimes. I just try to push the limits. If you can't really keep up with other cars, then it feels to you like you're still driving in first place.'

- After disappointment in Melbourne 2017: 'The most positive thing today? The weather.'
- On his overtaking race in Shanghai 2017: 'When I had already overtaken nine cars on the first lap, I thought I was playing a video game.'
- Again, Shanghai 2017: 'The wetter the track, the better for me and more exciting for you.'
- To Lewis Hamilton, who wasn't voted driver of the day in that race in China, he said: 'It's obviously much harder to get elected when you're at the front and not overtaking anyone... If you want to swap places, that's fine by me.'
- A Sky Sports reporter tried to appease him after Bahrain one year by saying Hamilton had become afraid of him. Max replies: 'Oh well, I don't know. I never had the chance to put pressure on him. He always controlled the gap. I just drove my race and it wasn't my intention to pass him. When I got close, he just drove away from me again. It was a game of cat and mouse.'
- On the weather in Bahrain: 'It's definitely not going to rain here.'
- About criticism of his driving style: 'I just take it as a compliment. I'm pretty easy about that. You'll always have that kind of thing. If you're new to a sport, you'll always have people criticising and complaining. All you can do is go your own way and do your best once you're in the car.'
- On overtaking in general: 'Successfully overtaking gives the same feeling as karting. The adrenaline and relief that goes through you are the same. The cars are bigger, but you know exactly what the dimension of the car is and how much space you need to stay on the tarmac.'
- Asked who he prefers, Lewis Hamilton or Sebastian Vettel: 'Neither.'
- His schooling: 'At school I had a notepad on which I just drew circuits.'
- If his parents had been teachers, would he have gone racing? 'Maybe not, but I definitely wouldn't have become a teacher.'
- About the Zandvoort race days, attended by tens of thousands of fans: 'They're harder than driving a race.'
- About the legendary corner names of Monaco, such as Rascasse and Massenet, which he doesn't know: 'Let's just call them turn one, two, three or six. Can't we?'
- During Monaco 2017 on the radio, referring to his team-mate: 'Did Daniel stop? What a fucking, fucking disaster.'
- In reply to criticism of his use of language on the radio: 'What should I say? Thanks guys?'

Zandvoort celebrations attended by tens of thousands of fans:
'They're harder than driving a race.'

- About leaving school at 15 to focus fully on motorsport: 'Many drivers have done the same. But if it doesn't work out, you have to go back to school and study. That was extra motivation for me to do my utmost. I've never thought about anything else but Formula 1.'
- On ambitions: 'If you don't care if you finish third or fifth, you don't belong in Formula 1.'
- Again, on criticism of his aggressive driving style: 'At the end of the day everyone is entitled to their own opinion. But at the end of the day that's what I am and that's what got me where I am today. So I see no reason to change.'
- On playing football: 'That didn't give me as much adrenaline as karting. You're always on the limit of what you can do.'
- On loyalty in Formula 1: 'I don't think it's normal, but it's always nice when you can give it. Red Bull gave me the chance in Formula 1, so loyalty definitely plays a role with me.'
- On the massive support from his fans at tracks like Red Bull Ring: 'I am just as relaxed at Spa as I am in Spain or Melbourne. It's not like having more home fans in the grandstand makes you go a tenth faster through the corners.'
- When asked by an English journalist if he's the fastest driver in the world: 'Hard to say. Maybe there's someone in Africa who's faster than me.'
- After his Red Bull's loss of power in Canada 2017, team principal Christian Horner said: 'Luckily his radio went out as well. I think his reaction would not have been good.' Afterwards Max still had the last word: 'It's been bad all season. With everything.'
- How to proceed: 'To be honest I don't care. It is what it is, but at the moment I have had enough. I just want to go home and, like after Monaco, try not to think about it. Just start again at the next race and see if we can at least finish.'
- After fast lap times during free practice in Azerbaijan: 'How I suddenly become so fast? A good night's sleep and 100 push-ups.'
- After his retirement at Azerbaijan in 2017: 'On Wednesday I have a simulator day. At least then the engine can't break down.'
- Responding to former driver Mark Webber's call to stop penalising drivers with grid penalties for technical problems that aren't their fault. 'Maybe it's an idea to impose fines on teams for technical faults. But then my team would be heading for bankruptcy.'

- On the announcement by Helmut Marko that Red Bull wouldn't let him go for €100 million amidst rumours that Ferrari wanted him: 'Maybe at 101 million it would happen. What's in it for me? Nothing. I just want to get results.'
- When he made a detour over the kerbs at Silverstone one year, Christian Horner said over the radio: 'Yellows at turn seven Max, yellows at turn seven.' He replied: 'Yeah, that was me, ha-ha-ha.'
- When asked if his 10-second penalty in Hungary 2017, dropping him from third to fifth place, was justified: 'I hit someone and they crashed out. Whether that penalty is too severe? That is not for me to decide.'
- After retirement in Austria: 'As a driver you always do your best. You just have to be lucky to be with the right team at the right time. Formula 1 has always been like that. You can only win with a good car. I knew that when I was six years old.'
- Before a contract renewal with Red Bull, in Singapore: 'We still have time. Otherwise I know a supermarket where I can work.' Dutch supermarket chain Jumbo is one of his sponsors.
- On all his frustrations through the first half of the 2018 season: 'Why I don't smash something, or throw something? That's how I was brought up. I have never been allowed to and never done that. If you lose the world title in the last race, yes, that's another story. But I am not in that situation. It's not resignation, but I just can't do anything about it.'
- Social media channels exploded after his second Grand Prix victory, in Malaysia in 2017. He even received congratulations from politicians, amongst others. 'It took me a while to respond to everyone. I also got more responses than after Barcelona last year. I have more friends now. I can't keep track of all that anymore.'
- The victory in Malaysia in 2017 was still no match for the best day of his career, 22nd September 2013, when he became the youngest-ever karting world champion in Varennes-sur-Allier, France: 'That's still my best victory... I worked so hard together with my father for that.'
- Over the on-board radio during that race, when he overtook World Champion Lewis Hamilton for the lead: 'That's how we do it.'
- On Hamilton's compliments after his second place in Japan in 2017: 'He is only nice when he wins.'
- That he knows something about history is shown by his reaction after visiting NASA in 2017 before the United States Grand Prix. After a

Monaco 2019: 'I drove 77 laps behind a grey Mercedes. The fact that
we have a few points is positive, let's leave it at that.'

simulated experience with weightlessness, he tweeted: 'That's one small step for a man, one giant leap for mankind.'

- On the suggestion of becoming second driver at Ferrari: 'If there's one thing I don't want, it's to end up as second driver somewhere. I'd rather quit.'
- About money: 'I'd rather win a hundred races for free than get a hundred million euros.'
- On his time penalty in America in 2017: 'This is not good for the sport. I really hope that next year no one will come here.'
- On politically correct answers: 'I think it is very important to say what I want. I don't want to hold back or lie. I am straightforward and I don't want to change that.'
- On his Mexican victory in 2017: 'Since I turned 20, everything is a lot easier.
- And: 'I thought, maybe I should cut a corner, then I get a five-second time penalty and maybe it will be exciting.'
- During the race, cruising along in the lead: 'Simply, simply wonderful.'
- In Brazil in 2017, after an enforced tyre change, he asked: 'How fast is the fastest lap?' Christian Horner replied: 'Too fast, Max.' Moments later he set the fastest lap (subsequently improved by Sebastian Vettel).
- On Helmut Marko, the stern Red Bull adviser: 'Helmut is a bit tougher than most people, but I've worked with my father all my life. There is nobody stricter and harder on me than he is.'
- Asked by his race engineer on one occasion how the track was, he replied: 'Sunny!'
- On the entire 2017 season: 'A missed opportunity. We had DNFs too often. It was also a learning year. I learned to stay positive at the difficult moments.'
- After finishing the 2019 Australian Grand Prix, the first race with the Honda engine, in third place: 'Everything has to be better if we want to beat our rivals.'
- On the impossibility of overtaking at Monaco in 2019: 'I drove 77 laps behind a grey Mercedes. The fact that we have a few points is positive, let's leave it at that.'
- On not observing what other teams do: 'You can only control what you can control.'
- Ignoring advice from the pits to preserve his tyres: 'I'm not here to finish fourth.'

Abu Dhabi 2021: 'My God, guys, I love you so much. Can we do this another 10 or 15 years together?'

- After Baku in 2019: 'It does get a bit boring to see Hamilton win so often.'
- During the 2019 Zandvoort race days: 'I daresay I haven't become a different person.'
- On strange requests from fans: 'Twice someone has asked me to autograph a passport. I don't know if it is allowed, but I did it. I just hope it was an expired passport.'
- On radio messages during the 2019 French Grand Prix: 'The tcam kept going: "Ferrari this, Mercedes that, lap times here, lap times there." I was like, 'Guys, I am not going any faster. I don't have a magic accelerator.'
- On the matter of revenge: 'In the end, not much good comes from being like that. I approach a weekend the way I approach every weekend: just relaxed. I'm up for it. I don't need to pep myself up or anything like that.'
- Reflecting on his third place in the World Championship points standings after the last race of 2019, in Abu Dhabi: 'When I look back on my career in 20 years' time, I don't think I will recall much about the third place.'
- Before the sensational race in Russia in 2021, where he started last and finished second, Hamilton had ramped up the pressure beforehand, stating that he was used to such situations but Max wasn't — to which the Dutchman responded. 'I'm so nervous I can't sleep. It's terrible to be fighting for a title.'
- Before the Turkish Grand Prix in 2021, answering a question about the title fight: 'I always give my best and I know my team does too. If that means we are first at the end of the year, it's a great achievement. But even if we end up second, we have had in my opinion a tremendous season, and at the end of the day my life won't be very different. I enjoy what I'm doing and that's also very important.'
- During 2021: 'If I have only one chance [to become World Champion) I would be very happy. Formula 1 is just one part of my life. Many people are too serious about Formula 1.'
- His cry of joy after winning the 2021 Abu Dhabi Grand Prix: 'My God, guys, I love you so much. Can we do this another 10 or 15 years together?'
- Interviewed on Dutch television a day after becoming World Champion: 'It doesn't change my life, but I am more relaxed now that I've achieved my goal.'

EPILOGUE
DOING IT HOW YOU CAN

When I was working full-time on a daily newspaper and the evening deadline was approaching, my editor, after reviewing everything, would cover his position with the words: 'If you can't do it how you want to do it, you have to do it how you can.'

Mindful of that pragmatic attitude, I started the first Dutch edition of this book about Max Verstappen in 2016.

It wasn't an entirely obvious endeavour to write a book about an 18-year-old youth. Initially, the story wasn't even supposed to be called a biography because, after all, how could anyone have experienced enough at that age to provide sufficient substance for a biography? Unsuspecting outsiders might have wondered justifiably about making all this fuss over a young Dutch bloke. Meanwhile, more than five years have passed and Max Verstappen has become an unprecedented phenomenon — and, finally, Formula 1 World Champion. The 2021 Dutch Grand Prix in Zandvoort provided decisive evidence that convinced even the greatest sceptics, at least amongst his countrymen. Max Verstappen is special. He really is.

This young man, then still 23, rallied virtually the entire nation, including its king. He single-handedly put an end to the lingering coronavirus depression that had gripped the Netherlands, like everywhere else, for a year and a half. He united the Dutch people under their orange colours in a realm of sport that — as I have pointed out several times in this book — had never been taken seriously within the dykes and behind the dunes. Add to that the typically Dutch trait of false modesty and Verstappen's path suddenly becomes very special.

In the Netherlands, heroes are often hoisted aloft upon shoulders only to be quickly dropped to the ground again when times change. Father Jos has experienced this. He was once his country's big motorsport hope — until he wasn't. And thereafter, he was so haunted by scandals and bad press that he could barely show his face in public. The tabloid press blew up every scandal into a storm, from a fight at a go-kart track to fiery bust-ups in his private life. The hero of the 1994 Hockenheim fire was relegated to the status of a troublemaker.

But Max... that would be a different story.

To finish first, first you have to finish. It has been the same when writing this book, in its original form for the audience in my country but, now, in this much-expanded version for fans all over the world. First I had to carefully pinpoint the dots and then try to connect them step by step.

This didn't happen automatically, above all because the Verstappen family refused to cooperate, even after repeated requests. What's more, they weren't keen on the idea of a book at all. Why did there have to be a book? He hadn't proved anything yet, had he?

Of course, he hadn't proved too much at that time — that was a truism. But the Verstappens and their entourage knew what they had in store.

Jos saw Max as 'the greatest talent that motor racing has ever seen'.

'Of course, every father says that,' he added, 'but I am wise enough not to keep saying it.'

Sometimes in life you intuitively feel that something is about to happen. A small group saw that with Max.

When he made his Formula 1 début at middle-ranking Toro Rosso in 2015, it wasn't earth-shattering news. What was significant, however, was his age. I absorbed everything about that season because there was something special in the air. I have been following Formula 1 all my life, ever since I knew there were four wheels on a car. The fact that my son's first word was *oto* (car) says a lot about the conversations at home.

As a Formula 1 reporter for the Dutch press agency GPD, I could follow the sport closely. I had to snatch that privilege from the jaws of failure, because motorsport in the Netherlands... well, 'serious' sports journalism wanted nothing to do with it. After all, it was little more than a polluting procession of spoiled brats in excessively expensive cars. Why send a journalist on costly trips all over the world for most of the year just to report on a so-called sport in which a German driver or a German team has been winning for years on end?

My years in the paddock were addictive. The long weekends, which lasted from early on a Friday to late on a Sunday night, flew by in the blink of an eye. Chasing the story, you felt the shimmer of life in the fast lane. Face to face with Michael Schumacher or Mika Häkkinen, stars mingling on the grid, encounters with flamboyant team owners like Flavio Briatore, who liked to stroll between the trucks and motorhomes with his latest trophy — preferably a Miss World — on his arms.

Searching the Formula 1 forest for the best stories, you soon got stuck in the undergrowth. In those days a journalist could quietly approach a footballer, even if he played for a top team, and get his personal telephone number. However, in Formula 1 back then, 20-plus years ago, such short-cuts had already been eliminated — everything went through press people, management or marketing agencies. An off-the-record chat with someone senior within a team for a research topic would quickly peter out. Even an interview with a junior mechanic for a back-of-the-grid team had to go through endless official channels. Great stories, which all journalists strive for to justify their existence, have always been plentiful in Formula 1, but the trouble was you couldn't land them anymore.

That was partly because Formula 1 became more and more complicated — and more difficult to interpret.

Of course, chess is difficult too. Former world champion Garry Kasparov once said he could see 13 moves ahead, and then went on to analyse the game comprehensibly and comprehensively for the chess community. A football match takes place before your eyes: you don't just follow the ball but also observe the movements of other players and see patterns unfold.

A lot of what matters in Formula 1 takes place largely out of sight, under the skin of the cars, in the factories and within computers. A Formula 1 car consists of thousands of parts, all of which have an intimate relationship with each other. As a mere journalist, there's a lot to know if you're to make sense of it all. A Formula 1 team consists of many hundreds of employees, each carrying out a specialised task. Even if one or two of them were to speak openly, there would often be no story. It's very difficult to pinpoint the causes of victory or defeat.

In the modern era of Formula 1, with all its data, television imagery and expert analysis, we're making some progress towards better understanding, but not much. The real secrets remain concealed.

Fortunately, we still have drivers.

The driver is the human factor that, with all his strengths and weaknesses, with all his quirks and antics, is the element that makes Formula 1 a sport. A driver makes mistakes, shows emotions, knows the differences between his rivals. In short, he's the human touch in a high-performance and supremely technical activity that wouldn't otherwise be a sport.

The Formula 1 driver is the hero or the loser, the man the public can identify with. He makes his decisions in milliseconds. He steers with precision, accelerates rapidly and brakes at the last moment. He alone makes the car move. He does to excess the things that we all do (or would like to do) when driving a car, especially when there's pleasure involved on a particularly appealing stretch of road without traffic. So that's where the stories lie. It's in the cockpit where the difference is made, regardless of all the technical and electronic wizardry accomplished by the designers. A driver can make or break a car. A driver can give a team wings or send it down the pecking order.

There is so-called scientific proof that a driver accounts for only 14 percent of a team's result. That's nerdy nonsense. The driver is 100 percent responsible for the result, due to the simple reason that he's at the controls. If the driver doesn't do well, the team has no chance.

Max Verstappen is living proof of that.

So, a book about the remarkable rise of a Dutch Formula 1 driver, even if he was still young, seemed sufficiently interesting and worthwhile at least to research, and then to write later.

But how do you do that when the management of the protagonist has built a wall of commercial interests around him?

Well, everywhere he went, the growing teenager left evidence behind him. The most significant insights were to be found at Van Amersfoort Racing. Frits van Amersfoort coached the young Verstappen in Formula 3 and is usually amenable about speaking to the media. Then there were the men of MP Motorsport and Paul Lemmens with his kart track in Genk where little Max first burned rubber. This is how the story began to slowly take shape.

And what else? Max Verstappen is an open book in the media. He's a child of the online generation and visible everywhere. There are a plenty of early interviews with the small, charming Max that I could also use.

Mission accomplished: Jos and Max share a few moments after
the 2021 Abu Dhabi Grand Prix.

EPILOGUE

When my Dutch publisher approached me on the question of whether I wanted to write this book, I first had to research where to find the necessary information and whose cooperation I could count on. I had already approached the family and they had indicated that they didn't want to cooperate. Then I contacted Huub Rothengatter.

Huub knew all the ins and outs. How the first contract negotiations went, how much he had invested in Max's career. He was on friendly terms with Jos and watched Max grow up. Huub is a nice guy but someone who operates on the principle of give and take. Huub has never done anything for nothing. I once managed to arrange an interview with him for the press agency I worked for at the time. After much urging, he agreed, but only if I offered something in return. I don't remember exactly what. In any case, it wasn't money, but probably some kind of publicity favour. In the case of Max's story, Huub and I drank coffee, talked about this and that, and renewed our acquaintance from years before. When he said he wouldn't cooperate, it felt like a cold shower.

Years ago, I wrote a book about the Dutch sports car manufacturer Spyker, which had ventured into Formula 1 (amongst other things). I treated the project like peeling an onion. Layer by layer, I unravelled the subject and slowly reached the core. The method is a handy journalistic tool. First the foot soldiers, then the sergeants — and finally you hope to reach the general. It worked very well. After I had spoken to many Spyker people, the CEO, Victor Muller, contacted me because he wanted to share his version of the story. That's how my Spyker book, *Langs de Afgrond* ('Along the Abyss'), came about and that's how I thought I could construct my book about Max. Only Max never called me...

Jos did.

The Spyker book, of course, was completely different. It was all about controversies, the financial battlefield, the theft of the brand, transferred bankruptcies, jealousy, the drama of the Le Mans 24 Hours, the ridiculous Formula 1 adventure... It was a boys' adventure story.

Max's story has also become a boys' book, but from a totally different angle. He lives the life that lots of little boys dream of. After all, most 10-year-old boys want to be pilots, footballers or Formula 1 drivers. Don't they?

And when all that fails, they become modest journalists who write about it.

If you can't do it how you want to do it, you have to do it how you can.

262

STATISTICS

Youngest first-time Grand Prix winners

Max Verstappen (NL)	18 years 226 days	2016	Spanish Grand Prix
Sebastian Vettel (D)	21 years 73 days	2008	Italian Grand Prix
Fernando Alonso (E)	22 years 26 days	2003	Hungarian Grand Prix
Bruce McLaren (NZ)	22 years 204 days	1959	United States Grand Prix
Lewis Hamilton (GB)	22 years 154 days	2007	Canadian Grand Prix
Kimi Räikkönen (SF)	23 years 157 days	2003	Malaysian Grand Prix
Robert Kubica (PL)	23 years 184 days	2008	Canadian Grand Prix
Jacky Ickx (B)	23 years 188 days	1968	French Grand Prix
Michael Schumacher (D)	23 years 240 days	1992	Belgian Grand Prix

Youngest World Champions

Sebastian Vettel (D)	23 years 13 days	2010
Lewis Hamilton (GB)	23 years 300 days	2008
Fernando Alonso (E)	24 years 57 days	2005
Max Verstappen (NL)	24 years 73 days	2021
Emerson Fittipaldi (BR)	25 years 273 days	1972

Max's 'youngest' records

Grand Prix start	17 years 166 days	2015	Australian Grand Prix
Grand Prix points	17 years 180 days	2015	Malaysian Grand Prix
Grand Prix winner	18 years 228 days	2016	Spanish Grand Prix
Grand Prix podium	18 years 228 days	2016	Spanish Grand Prix
Leading a Grand Prix	18 years 228 days	2016	Spanish Grand Prix
Grand Prix fastest lap	19 years 44 days	2016	Brazilian Grand Prix
Grand Slam*	23 years 277 days	2021	Austrian Grand Prix

Pole position, fastest lap, victory, leading all race laps

FIA Formula 1 World Championship summary (2015–21)

Year	Position	Points	Races	Wins	Podiums	Poles	Fastest laps
2015	12th	49	19	0	0	0	0
2016	5th	204	21	1	7	0	1
2017	6th	168	20	2	4	0	1
2018	4th	249	21	2	11	0	2
2019	3rd	278	21	3	9	2	3
2020	3rd	214	17	2	11	1	3
2021	1st	395.5	22	10	18	10	6

Grand Prix wins (2016–21)

2016	Spanish Grand Prix (Catalunya)
2017	Malaysian Grand Prix (Sepang)
	Mexican Grand Prix (Mexico City)
2018	Austrian Grand Prix (Red Bull Ring)
	Mexican Grand Prix (Mexico City)
2019	Austrian Grand Prix (Red Bull Ring)
	German Grand Prix (Hockenheimring)
	Brazilian Grand Prix (Interlagos)
2020	70th Anniversary Grand Prix (Silverstone)
	Abu Dhabi Grand Prix (Yas Marina)
2021	Emilia Romagna Grand Prix (Imola)
	Monaco Grand Prix (Monte Carlo)
	French Grand Prix (Le Castellet)
	Styrian Grand Prix (Red Bull Ring)
	Austrian Grand Prix (Red Bull Ring)
	Belgian Grand Prix (Spa-Francorchamps)
	Dutch Grand Prix (Zandvoort)
	United States Grand Prix (Austin)
	Mexican Grand Prix (Mexico City)
	Abu Dhabi Grand Prix (Yas Marina)

Grand Prix placings (2015–21)

1st	20
2nd	25
3rd	15
4th	14
5th	12
6th	5
7th	2
8th	6
9th	5
10th	3
Others	7
DNF	27
Total	**141**

Other Grand Prix statistics (2015–21)

Pole positions	13
Fastest laps	16
Races led	39
Laps led	1,205
Distance led	3,493 miles (5,622km)

FIA European Formula 3 Championship summary

Year	Position	Points	Races	Wins	Podiums	Poles	Fastest laps
2014	3rd	411	33	10	16	7	7

Florida Winter Series summary

Year	Position	Points	Races	Wins	Podiums	Poles	Fastest laps
2014	–	–	12	2	5	3	3

Karting victories

2006	Rotax Max Challenge Belgium (Mini Max)
2007	Dutch Championship (Rotax Mini Max)
	Rotax Max Challenge Belgium National (Mini Max)
	Rotax Max Challenge Belgium (Mini Max)
2008	Belgian Championship (Cadet)
	Rotax Max Challenge Belgium (Mini Max)
	Benelux Karting Series (Mini Max)
2009	VAS Championship (Rotax Mini Max)
	Belgian Championship (KF5)
	Benelux Karting Series (Mini Max)
2010	WSK Euro Series (KF3)
	Bridgestone Cup European Final (KF3)
	WSK World Series (KF3)
	WSK Nations Cup (KF3)
2011	WSK Euro Series (KF3)
2012	South Garda Winter Cup (KF2)
	WSK Master Series (KF2)
2013	South Garda Winter Cup (KF2)
	WSK Euro Series (KF1)
	WSK Master Series (KZ2)
	CIK-FIA European Championship (KF)
	CIK-FIA European Championship (KZ)
	CIK-FIA World Championship (KZ)

PHOTO CREDITS

Alamy 46, 53, 55, 66, 75, 79, 81, 112, 129, 173, 198–199, 249,
Getty Images 19, 97, 115, 119, 136, 207, 245, front cover
Motorsport Images 4, 10, 14–15, 25, 26, 32, 35, 36, 39, 43, 49, 58, 63, 65, 71, 87, 92, 123, 124, 126–127, 135, 144–145, 147, 152, 157, 160–161, 167, 168, 171, 179, 181, 185, 189, 194, 203, 208, 215, 218, 220–221, 228, 231, 232–233, 237, 242–243, 252, 254, 261, back cover
Will Buxton 103, 107

INDEX

INDEX

THE AUTHOR

André Hoogeboom is a Dutch journalist and writer specialising in Formula 1, and currently runs his own press and consultancy agency. His unauthorised biography of Max Verstappen was first published in the Netherlands in 2016 and has now been much expanded and adapted to bring it up to date and to suit English-speaking audiences. His other books about motorsport include a history of Zandvoort (his country's premier racetrack), a reconstruction of the adventures of Dutch car manufacturer Spyker (including its short-lived Formula 1 experience), and two novels, *Deadly Ambition* and *Sabotage*. He lives in Alkmaar, near Amsterdam.